EDITH WHARTON: TRAVELLER IN THE LAND OF LETTERS

Edith Wharton

Traveller in the Land of Letters

Janet Goodwyn

St. Martin's Press   New York

© Janet Patricia Goodwyn 1990

First published in the United States of America in 1990

Printed in Hong Kong

ISBN 0–312–03200–5

Library of Congress Cataloging-in-Publication Data
Goodwyn, Janet, 1956–
Edith Wharton : traveller in the land of letters / Janet Goodwyn.
     p.   cm.
Bibliography: p.
Includes index.
ISBN 0–312–03200–5
1. Wharton, Edith, 1862–1937—Criticism and interpretation.
I. Title.
PS3545.H16Z655   1990
813'.52—dc19   89–6050
                                                           CIP

#19395229

For my parents, with love

Contents

Contents

Acknowledgements

The author and publishers wish to thank the following for permission to quote from the work of Edith Wharton:

The Collection of American Literature, Beinecke Rare Book and Manuscript Library, Yale University;

Watkins/Loomis Agency Inc., New York, for excerpts from *A Backward Glance* (New York: 1934; reprinted by Constable & Co., 1972).

I would also like to thank everyone who has helped me with my work on Edith Wharton, both in England and the United States, and particularly the staff of the Yale Beinecke Library, 1980–1981. My special thanks are due to John Stokes, who saw my work through its academic process; to my husband, Andrew Goodwyn, who has shared his home with Edith Wharton for a decade and can still express enthusiasm for her; to Marion Maidment, for her love and support; and, finally, to my son, Thomas Goodwyn, for being a sound sleeper.

                                                                Janet Goodwyn

Introduction

Edith Wharton's first novel, *The Valley of Decision*, was published in 1902, a month after her fortieth birthday. For the child who used to cover the brown wrapping paper from her mother's Paris dresses with closely written stories and pace about her bedroom, upside-down text in hand, declaiming her own fictions to the walls, this belated publication marked a definitive change of life. Wharton had been in print before 1902: a small volume of poetry, two collections of short stories, a treatise on interior design co-written with the architect, Ogden Codman, and a novella. All these preceded *The Valley of Decision*, but it was the novel which truly marked her entry into the world of the professional writer.

This 'romantic chronicle'[1] as Wharton called her first novel, was an experiment which she never repeated; never again did she venture so far into the past nor so deep into another country without an American cast of characters. However, the processes of composition of the book, the background reading and organisation of historical material, proved to be an invaluable exercise for the aspiring novelist, especially when looked at in conjunction with the writing of her two Italian travel books, *Italian Villas and Their Gardens*, published in 1904, and *Italian Backgrounds*, 1905. Her successful apprenticeship in the short story combined with her skills as observer and recorder in the guidebooks provided an inspirational beginning for an artist whose work would always be distinguished by its innovative use of specific landscapes and its topographical coherence.

Wharton thought of her fiction as possessing a particular geography and from the time of publication of *The Valley of Decision* onwards she was to regard the plying of the written word as much more than her profession; in fact, her art became her place of residence; as she says in her published autobiography, *A Backward Glance*:

> I felt like some homeless waif who, after trying for years to take out naturalization papers, and being rejected by every country, has finally acquired a nationality. The Land of Letters was henceforth to be my country and I gloried in my new citizenship.[2]

1

The extended metaphor taken by Wharton to describe her confirmation as a writer is of central importance to the subject matter and form of the whole body of her fiction as well as to her own sense of belonging in 'The Land of Letters'. Throughout her writing life she was concerned with ideas of place: the American's place in the Western world, the woman's place in her own and in European society, the author's place in the larger life of a culture. She experimented with settings, with time, with genres, seeking to illuminate the lives of her characters and, in the travel books, enlighten her readers, with geographical and cultural differences. From *The Valley of Decision* to *The Buccaneers*, her last, unfinished novel, the various and many landscapes of Wharton's fiction whether actual or, as above, metaphorical, give structure and point to the text.

In this study of Edith Wharton's work I propose to shape my discussion by use of her specific landscapes. Not only did she set her novels in a variety of countries, she made the cultural imperatives of those lands reference points in her fictions. The landscapes are separate but they are also complementary. Wharton's sense of the unity of culture between America and Europe, the way in which one landscape can suggest another, illuminate another, enhance appreciation of another, is constantly a theme in both her fiction and travel writing.

Wharton herself was a perpetual tourist; no sooner did she return from one trip than she was planning the next. She owned one of the first automobiles and was convinced, as she declares at the opening of *A Motor-Flight Through France*, that 'The motor-car has restored the romance of travel'.[3] She used both her literary earnings and her inherited income to finance her tours, her peripatetic childhood having equipped her with a facility, and later a fluency, in all the major European languages. Travel both fed her imagination and restored her to a sense of self-possession; her experiences as a tourist fuelled her life as a writer.

I found a clue to the enlightening possibilities of a topographical approach to critical discussion of Wharton's work in her travel writings, the guides to foreign cultures which she offered to her American audience. The two Italian books – *Italian Villas and Their Gardens* and *Italian Backgrounds* – illuminate the novel, *The Valley of Decision*, just as the French books – *A Motor-Flight Through France* (1908), *Fighting France from Dunquerque to Belfort* (1915) and *French Ways and Their Meaning* (1919) – extend and vivify the novels which are set partly or wholly in France. In times of peace and of war Wharton made the landscape and society of France act as counterpoint to a largely American cast of characters.

The group of novels and travelogues which are distinguished by their concern with French civilisation, in its broadest sense, mark a time of transition in Wharton's work which actually mirrors the larger whole-cultural upheavals of the period. From the novella, *Madame de Treymes*, published in 1907, to *A Son at the Front*, finally published in 1923, the focus of Wharton's writing moves from a Europe of romance, viewed by the privileged aesthete-tourist and communicated to an audience with little or no firsthand experience of foreign travel, to a Europe made familiar to the United States by war and already, as Gertrude Stein would have it,[4] left behind by America's declaration of the new cultural boundaries of the twentieth century. The European subject treated as the prehistory of her own country in *The Valley of Decision* is transmuted in Wharton's writing by gradations. The gentle transatlanticism of the Americans in *Madame de Treymes* and her 1912 novel, *The Reef*, gives way to the acultural plundering of the European continent by such as Undine Spragg, the central character of *The Custom of the Country*, (1913).

Not only is a topographical grouping of Wharton's work critically enlightening in consideration of those books set in France and Italy but it is most revelatory in examination of the rôle of her native, American landscape. In the novel sequence which I take to be concerned with her own country, Wharton experiments with and comments upon modes of American narrative through both structure and theme. To read the novels *The House of Mirth* (1904), *The Fruit of the Tree* (1907), *Ethan Frome* (1911), *Summer* (1917), *The Glimpses of the Moon* (1922), *The Mother's Recompense* (1925), *Twilight Sleep* (1927), and *The Children* (1928) as a distinct American group provides a native context in which to place her work. The specific cultural portraiture which distinguishes her French and Italian writing takes on a different character in the books and articles which focus on the American scene. A changing New York is Wharton's primary subject; in her fiction she signals the end of a topographical certainty which had endured for three hundred years. As she says in *A Backward Glance*:

Not until the successive upheavals which culminated in the catastrophe of 1914 had 'cut all likeness from the name' of my old New York, did I begin to see its pathetic picturesqueness. The first change came in the 'eighties, with the earliest detachment of big money-makers from the West, soon to be followed by the lords of Pittsburgh. But their infiltration did not greatly affect old manners and customs, since the dearest ambition of the newcomers was to assimilate existing traditions. Social life, with us as in the rest of the world, went on with hardly perceptible changes till the war abruptly tore down the old frame-work, and what had seemed unalterable rules of conduct became of a sudden observances as quaintly arbitrary as the domestic rites of the Pharoahs. Between the point of view of my Huguenot great-great-grandfather, who came from the French Palatinate to participate in the founding of New Rochelle, and my own father, who died in 1882, there were fewer differences than between my father and the post-war generation of Americans.[5]

She reacts, in her novels, to the removal of the inherited securities and values of her nineteenth-century upbringing; she makes a vital connection between the cultural situation of early American writers – who had to invent their own fictional landscapes – and the coming generation – who would be forced to deal with the dislocation of twentieth- from nineteenth-century America.

A crucial convergence of influence and circumstance make Edith Wharton the key articulator of turn-of-the-century America: not only did her upbringing amongst the first New York families provide her with the sharpest personal insight into the transactions between old and new cultural conditions, but, as a woman, she was at the heart of current artistic concern. The writers of the age, from Henry Adams to Sinclair Lewis, are not only concerned with the prerogatives of American commercial and political life, but with the conditions created by the absence of the male from the other part of the culture and the fact that the women of America are the creators and arbiters of the social scene. Wharton's writing proves to be an invaluable bridge between American fiction of the nineteenth and twentieth centuries, between Henry James and F. Scott Fitzgerald, shedding light on the past whilst also showing the way forward. I have been able, in recognising the homology of the novels which have at their heart the changing, constantly disintegrating and restructuring American scene, to make a radical re-reading of the novels of the 1920s – novels substantially ignored by critics in the past – and also a reassessment of their relationship to Wharton's other, better-known works.

Wharton's confidence in the cultural significance of topography, as expressed through the various landscapes of her fiction, does take a slightly different form in her autobiographical work. From 1912 onwards she was experimenting with several modes of self-presentation, both direct and indirect; the texts concerned with her residence in 'The Land of Letters' display differing degrees of autobiographical involvement and are in various stages of composition, some completed, some not. She began an auto-biography, 'Life and I', probably around 1912, which remained incomplete, and published a formal autobiography, *A Backward Glance*, in 1934. This official autobiography – official because made public by Wharton as the authorised version of her life – has always been considered something of a disappointment because of its reticence and its reluctance to contend with the complexities of structure and expression attendant upon the retrospective view. A broader picture of her life and the influences which shaped her can be gained, however, if we read the various autobiographies and those experiences which she translated into the fictional life of a character called Richard Thaxter in the unfinished novel, 'Litera-ture', in the manner of a palimpsest. The formal autobiography is the top layer of the portrait and the other writings lie underneath it in various forms which can then be read in their intertextual relation. *A Backward Glance* was the last full-length work published in Wharton's lifetime and as such it sets a seal on her previous writings. The seal can nevertheless be broken – and indeed Wharton must have intended that it should when she left her unfinished work to be read by a later generation – by reading backwards through the self-portraits. The autobiographical process is further illuminated, though not in so direct a self-referencing manner, in the novels, *Hudson River Bracketed* and *The Gods Arrive*. Here the fictional landscape is treated in terms of its specific effect on the writer, Vance Weston, of Euphoria, Illinois. Unlike Richard Thaxter, who shares the same kind of upbringing as Wharton, Vance is distanced from her own background, but from this point of difference she then proceeds to expose him to a number of the same influences which she felt crucial to her own development in order to explore, yet again, the making of the artist.

In many ways Wharton's building-up of creative confidence through a definition of landscape comes to fruition in her historical novel writing, the mode to which she returned in 1920 with *The Age of Innocence*. She could bring all her topographical expertise to bear upon the New York of her childhood; the landscape of memory conjoining the well charted landscape of the novel to produce *The Age of Innocence, Old New York,* (1924) and *The Buccaneers,* (1938). Where travel and research had illuminated the background for her only other historical novel, *The Valley of Decision,* the topography of these stories is her own and is therefore directly recollectable. Here Wharton assumes the past in full consciousness of her power to recreate and, crucially, to explore, the conditions of her youth; she writes in a freely discursive mode, a mode which is distinct from the inevitably more self-protective and conservative approach of her final autobiographical reclamations of the past in *A Backward Glance*.

With the exception of *A Son at the Front* (1923), the last novel in which she was directly concerned with the first world war, all her work, from *The Age of Innocence* onwards, is taken up with the difficulties of placing the American, of marking out a specifically American topography. Faced with what George Frenside, a character from her novel, *Hudson River Bracketed,* calls the 'after-war welter, with its new recipe for immortality every morning',[6] Wharton turned to the nineteenth century which, in 1920, seemed to her almost as another country. The historical background of the post-war world was now as much American as European and it became possible for Wharton to write, amongst other things, a true historical novel set in her own land. As the two continents of Europe and North America entered the new century together, Wharton could express the vanished New York of the 1870s in *The Age of Innocence* in the language of social anthropology – now applicable to the American for the first time – as the last traces of the world she depicts have receded from view.

In the forty years during which Wharton was publishing her work the relationship between Europe and the United States went through a sea-change. Not only was the Atlantic diminished as a barrier for voyagers but the balance of power moved from one side of the ocean to the other. The entry of America into the war was also the entry of the American into all corners of Europe and Edith Wharton's fiction, in its breadth and its concerns, paints a picture of the reversal of the relationship of authority and influence. Her landscapes reflect the locus of power, whether east, west or mid-Atlantic, and her characters the personal and cultural effects of a shifting centre. She began, in *The Valley of Decision*, with the period leading up to the invasion of Italy by Napoleon. A civilisation was about to give way to an invader and she details the social conditions which made such an upheaval possible, an exercise that was to occupy her for the rest of her creative life.

1

The Valley of Decision

Wharton's choice of subject for her first full-length fiction – the Italian eighteenth century – enabled her to establish, for herself, a writer's sense of the importance of place, both historical and geographical, and also a sense of her own relation to other artists, other cultures. Writing about a period of great social change at a distance from her own personal experience in *The Valley of Decision*, she was actually empowered to formulate a coherent idea of her own situation as an artist, and particularly as a woman artist, in turn-of-the-century America.

To begin in a genre, a period, a country, a style which were all foreign to her actually eased the personal and artistic uncertainties attendant upon the transition between short story and novel writing for Wharton. The programme of reading and research which she undertook before beginning the novel, a process of preparation unique in her work, is revealing of her wish to put up a barrier of scholarship between herself and her audience. It was too early to expose herself as a creator personally involved in the lives of her subjects; that would come in her next novel, *The House of Mirth*, (1905), which was set in contemporary America amidst her own people. In writing of Odo Valsecca, heir to the Duchy of Pianura, and his mistress, the intellectual Fulvia Vivaldi, whose stories unfold hundreds of miles and years away from her, she drew on the writings of others and the experience of her own travels to set her scene, describing a country the geography of which was unknown to the majority of her readers.

The choice of subject she made is also revealing of something which is both fundamental and enduring in Wharton's work: the desire to act as a cross-cultural mediator. In this instance, she was purveying the Italian eighteenth century, which she perceived as having been neglected by scholars who were interested only in the art and architecture of France in this period, to a North American audience largely unfamiliar with either the history or the actual landscape of that country. Wharton's career opened and closed with an historical novel and the Italian past represented for her, at the outset, the wider cultural setting and background of her work. She needed to place herself as an American within the context of a shared history of Europe in order to realise her potential and power as an artist. The neglect of the Italian eighteenth century by scholars did not mean that there had been a lack of interest in the country by her compatriots: there was, in fact, a strong American precedent for Wharton to follow. Writing about Italy was a part of the process of grafting herself onto what she saw as a literary ancestral tree, 'the great genealogical tree of the arts' as she calls it in an unfinished essay 'Italy Again'.[1] No artistic tradition existed in her own family where writers were considered to be beyond the social pale: 'In the eyes of our provincial society authorship was still regarded as something between a black art and a form of manual labour'.[2]

Wharton was, however, fortunate in the scholarly friends and acquaintances to whom her social position allowed her access and in the breadth of her own background reading in the Italian subject, rare texts being made available to her by such as the Harvard professor, Charles Eliot Norton, whose own book, *Notes of Travel and Study in Italy*, had been published in 1859. Whether as tourists, historians or romancers, her compatriots had lingered over nineteenth-century Italy and had communicated their various impressions of the culture to an American audience. Her 'precursors',[3] to borrow Henry James's term for those who ante-dated his own venture into the Italian scene, provided Wharton with a starting-point from which to develop her own ideas on the presentation of her subject. American writers like Nathaniel Hawthorne in *The Marble Faun*, (1860), Henry Blake Fuller in *The Chevalier of Pensieri-Vani*, (1890), and William Dean Howells in *A Foregone Conclusion*, (1892), had combined, in distinct ways and with varying degrees of success, fiction with the guidebook. Wharton wrote in both genres, her first travel book, *Italian Villas and Their Gardens*, which arose from a commission from the *Century* magazine, was published in 1904, and her second, *Italian Backgrounds*, in 1905. But the two modes of presenting Italy, the factual and the fictional, are constantly and fruitfully in dialogue in her work; techniques and ideas interchange between the two and her writing is organised so as to put the cultural and historical differences which she sought to communicate to her primarily North American audience in the foreground of her picture.

It was not only from her American literary predecessors, however, that Wharton was able to gain inspiration for her Italian story: Madame de Staël's *Corinne, or Italy*, (1883), George Eliot's *Romola*, (1863), and Sir Walter Scott's *Waverley*, (1814), all these exercised Wharton's imagination and stimulated creative thinking on the particular problems of structuring an historical narrative. She was extensively and constructively influenced by all three authors. In *Corinne* and in *Romola* she found a precedent for the creation of a strong, intellectual woman of a type which could only be found in civilisations which – unlike the Anglo-Saxon – did not inhibit the woman's free social development, such as the Italy of de Staël or the France of Wharton's novels and guidebooks; and in Scott she found the example of a hero who occupies the middle ground, acting as a barometer for the currents of the age, reflecting them but never able himself to effect real change.

The central protagonist in *The Valley of Decision*, Odo Valsecca, in the line of succession of, and then incumbent of, the Dukedom of Pianura, a northern Italian state, is our guide through eighteenth-century Italy. As he is educated in the ways and means of his compatriots, so is his audience; he travels throughout the country, takes part in archaeological investigations, fraternises with poets and philosophers, poor farmers, powerful Dukes and Princes, strolling-players and priests. Through his eyes we see the complex problems of a post-feudal society still organised on feudal lines but we also see the terrible incapacity of Odo or any of his contemporaries to integrate the forces of change into the existing or any kind of new social order. Under the influence of his mistress, Fulvia Vivaldi, described by the radical poet, Alfieri, in the novel as 'one of your prodigies of female learning, such as our topsy-turvy land produces',[4] Odo seeks to implement certain ill-fated reforms, and in particular the restriction of the influence of the church upon the state. It is this latter ambition which directly causes the failure of the new constitution, as the church is able to inspire enough public feeling against the reforms to provoke a rebellion. Fulvia is shot dead by a protester and Odo, overcome by this loss and by the general reaction to his work, is ultimately forced, by the liberal faction which first inspired him, to surrender to the invading forces of Napoleon.

The story as outlined here is always, however, secondary to Wharton's wider ambitions in the novel as her intention was primarily to draw a picture of an age, a landscape humanised by centuries of civilisation – from the achievements of the Ancient Romans to those of the eighteenth century – and now in the midst of a period of great social change. Wharton felt entirely comfortable with this combination of fiction and pedagogy and had found a precedent for such writing in Madame de Staël's work in the Italian subject. As Ellen Moers says in her book, *Literary Women*, 'The oddest thing about *Corinne* is that it is a guidebook to Italy just as much as it is a guidebook to the woman of genius. Madame de Staël called the novel *Corinne, or Italy* to signify its double usefulness'.[5] Wharton's novel, in common with de Staël's, has a dual didactic intent, as a guide for the tourist to the Italian landscape, and additionally, as a guide to the possibilities contained within it for the woman.

In many respects Wharton, and before her George Eliot, wrote as an academic tourist in the Italian subject. Both women, late and uncertain starters in their careers as novelists, worked hard amongst documents of the period – although Wharton strenuously denied having undertaken such preparations in her later autobiographical writing – and the novels are ultimatly testaments to their reading rather than their writing skills. Gordon Haight, in his *George Eliot: A Biography*, describes Eliot's work in the Maglibecchian library: 'Here Marion copied into her notebook information about the Florence of Savonarola's day – costume, language, etymologies of names, descriptions of fairs and ceremonies, jesters, barbers, matchmakers, street-lighting, bonfires, games, the making and marketing of woollen cloth'.[6] Wharton's 'Writer's Notebook' for *The Valley of Decision* contains lists of phrases, cosmetics, clothing and details of secular and social practices in the Italy of the time most of which find their way directly into the text.

The characterisation of Romola herself within Eliot's novel, and of Fulvia Vivaldi in Wharton's story – their motherlessness, their positions as intellectual handmaidens to their respective fathers, their strength of mind in combination with an active compassion – these are all either imitative of or developments of de Staël's portrait of Corinne. The emphasis which is placed on Corinne's skill as an improviser, a performing artist, is converted in Fulvia Vivaldi to her skill, under-used though it may be, in political oratory. More straightforwardly renewed, however, is the failure of romantic love to match up to the expectations of the exceptional woman; as Corinne loses the man she loves because of her commitment to the opportunities offered to her by the Italian scene, her desire to live a personal life which is in concert, not conflict, with the wider demands and expectations of society, so Fulvia: 'had chosen to be regarded as a symbol rather than a woman, and there were moments when she felt as isolated from life as some marble allegory in its niche above the market-place'.[7] Even in Italy there is a high price to be paid for the difference between these 'prodigies of female learning' and other women of the time, but the nature of the choices they are forced to make shows how exact – much more so than in the case of the man – a reflection of cultural conditions are the lives of women. The topographical, here and throughout Wharton's work in all her various landscapes, is an enlightening measure of the female situation.

The doubts and misgivings which assailed Wharton, and before her George Eliot, in the composition of the historical novel, doubts evidenced by their extensive researches in the subject if nothing else, are equally the reason for their choice of subject matter and symptomatic of it. Elaine Showalter, in her book, *A Literature of Their Own*, singles out *Romola*, and Eliot's excessive preparations for its writing, as an illustration of general shamefastness or anxiety in women concerning their lack of education or simple ability to write: 'The danger of such strenuous self-cultivation lay in over-doing scholarship and becoming pedantic. George Eliot recognized this danger, as the figure of Casaubon [in *Middlemarch*] shows, but she could not help overcompensating in a book like *Romola*; in fact Romola's dedication to the preservation of her father's library is a paradigm of the feminine novelist's veneration of male culture. Other women novelists, too, felt compelled to bury themselves in research as a defense against accusations of ignorance'.[8] The act of research then is a strategy of self-protection; better to make a display of pedantry than to expose one's efforts to charges of ignorance and ridicule. Wharton always denied that her researches for the *The Valley of Decision* were anything more than 'the gradual absorption into my pores of a myriad details – details of landscape, architecture, old furniture and eighteenth-century portraits, the gossip of contemporary diarists and travellers, all vivified by repeated spring wanderings',[9] but in other contexts she never ceased to bemoan her lack of formal education. She blamed her parents for denying her the discipline of systematic study: 'Being deprived of the irreplaceable grounding of Greek and Latin, I never learned to concentrate except on subjects naturally interesting to me, and developed a restless curiosity which prevented my

fixing my thoughts for long even on these'.[10] Despite such express-
ions of deprivation, however, Wharton is vehement in dissociating
herself from techniques like those used by George Eliot in the
historical novel, techniques which she viewed as too formal and
academic; for instance, in the notes towards a piece – never
completed – called 'Fiction and Criticism':

> But the writer who deals with the past – who asks his reader to
> go with him to that land of mystery beyond the Chinese wall of
> the French revolution – has a more difficult feat to accomplish.
> For our conception of the men and women who lived three or
> four hundred years ago is made up not from personal experi-
> ence, but from literature and art – from the books they wrote, the
> pictures they painted and the houses they lived in. From the
> books we obtain, with more or less effort of mental adjustment, a
> notion of what they thought and how they expressed their ideas;
> but much more immediate and vivid is the notion formed of
> them from their appearance and environment. And it is for this
> reason that the visualizing gift is of the first importance to the
> historical novelist. George Eliot did not possess it. Her letters
> from Italy show her curious insensibility to qualities of atmos-
> phere, to values of form and colour. And for this reason her
> Florence, for all its carefully studied detail, remains a paste-
> board performance, like one of those reconstructions of medieval
> streets which are a popular feature of modern Exhibitions. Mr.
> Leslie Stephen, in his recent book on George Eliot, humorously
> complains that a certain article of dress called a scarsella gets on
> his nerves when he reads *Romola*. It is in fact a trick of the
> non-visualising novelist to attempt such archaeological details of
> dress and language to produce the effect which is not
> produced.[11]

The charges which Wharton makes against Eliot in this critique
are, ironically, those which she consistently addressed in her own
apologias for the writing of *The Valley of Decision*. She assumes a
potentially hostile critic – 'I did not travel and look and read with
the writing of the book in mind; but my years of intimacy with the
Italian eighteenth century gradually and imperceptibly fashioned
the tale and compelled me to write it'[12] – rebutting accusations of a
too scholarly approach before they are made. There are, nevertheless, several points of similarity between *Romola* and *The Valley of*

Decision, the defensive strain of Wharton's writing perhaps showing her to be aware of this. This fact of likeness, however, is not
necessarily indicative of weakness in either novel since, for instance, one of the devices selected by Wharton to highlight Eliot's
failure, the use of 'archaeological details', is also a significant part
of her strength and of Wharton's own, being intimately bound up
with both authors' strategy for communicating the Italian subject.

The historical novel, as practised by Eliot and Wharton, is
supported by the use of archaisms and figurative language. The
process of constructing 'that land of mystery beyond the Chinese
wall of the French revolution' relies extensively on the effective
selection of the representative detail from the mass of researched
or even – to use Wharton's preferred word – 'absorbed' information. The 'scarsella' which Stephen and Wharton find so irritating
is perhaps used a little insistently in *Romola*, as is the 'white hood'
which is designated as the signifying feature of the Florentine
contadina, but the specification of the item of dress performs
various functions; it denotes status, establishes a feature of the
social order and also reveals something of character in the way in
which it is worn. Similarly Wharton's mention of Odo's mistress's
request that he should bring her 'one of the rare lap-dogs bred by
the monks of Bologna'[13] passes an effective comment on the
interdependent values of church and aristocracy. This employment of synecdochic detail, although in some cases speaking only
of the writer's thoroughness of research, is generally successful in
evoking the spirit of the age, and this success is repeated in the use
of figurative language and in the method of characterisation,
particularly in *The Valley of Decision*.

The individuals whose lives concern us centrally in these novels
can be seen as emblematic representatives of their age in so far as
they signify forms of compromise. Neither Romola nor Odo,
despite intellectual and practical concern and great efforts on
Odo's part, is a successful creator of history. Wharton makes
repeated reference to Odo's fear of active engagement with his
time; despite the fact that history is 'being written, chapter by
chapter, before [his] very eyes', he is 'afraid to turn the next
page'.[14] Odo and Romola, like the protagonists of Sir Walter Scott's
novels designated by the critic Georg Lukács, in his book *The
Historical Novel*, as 'middle-of-the-road heroes',[15] can be seen to
reflect both sides of any question. Romola is pulled in one direction
by her father's secular scholarship and in the other by the

devotional demands of Savonarola and her brother. Odo Valsecca is intellectually drawn to the philosophy of the Vivaldis and the reforming spirit of Carlo Gamba, but feels the attractions of the hedonistic lifestyle of the aristocracy as well. His loyalties and instincts are divided: 'the stealing sense of duality that so often paralyzed his action'.[16] and it is only Fulvia's single-minded commitment to reform that takes the new constitution as far as it goes. Odo and Romola both live in a time coincident with great social change – surely a prerequisite for the writing of a successful historical novel which must stand out against present realities – and they give way, just as the 'intelligent amateur', the dying breed of tourist whom Wharton commemorates in 'Italy Again', is forced to give way before the professionals, whether writers of guide-books, politicians, philosophers, artists or priests.

In her Italian travel books, to which I will return later in a fuller discussion, Wharton makes central issue of the tendency of the Italian landscape to divide, for the observer, naturally but distinctively into two parts, foreground and background. She takes this topographical phenomenon and uses it to great effect in the structure of her Italian novel. Whilst those in the foreground, Odo and Fulvia, sometimes fall victim to the weight – whether of confusion or conviction – which they have to bear, the supporting characters who make up the background, are entirely effective in rounding-out the otherwise inaccessible details of the mundane existences against which the central protagonists must stand in relief. Odo, heir or Duke, is the locus for the philosophical, political and religious anxieties which agitate a whole country or even a whole continent, and his receptiveness to the different sides of every question, in the best Scott tradition, keeps him from being subsumed into the background, which is peopled by well defined types or representatives of local colour. The courtiers, the strolling players, the peasant farmers and clerics animate the general setting whilst the outstanding types, Trescorre, the time-serving politician, de Crucis, the pragmatic priest, Gamba, the radical and 'victim of the conditions he denounced',[17] and the Duchess, the aristocratic hedonist, carry a burden of signification sharpened by their proximity to and influence upon Odo himself. The structures of existence, analysed by a disillusioned Odo towards the end of his reign, are expressed by the classes which represent them:

Certainly in the ideal state the rights and obligations of the different classes would be more evenly adjusted. But the ideal state was a figment of the brain. The real one, as Crescenti had long ago pointed out, was the gradual and heterogeneous product of remote social conditions, wherein every seeming inconsistency had its roots in some bygone need, and the character of each class, with its special passions, ignorances and prejudices, was the sum total of influences so ingrown and inveterate that they had become a law of thought.[18]

Here is expounded not only the intent which has guided Wharton's choice and use of characters in the novel but also the whole-cultural motivation behind her work in the Italian historical subject. Each individual realises the sum of a particular social development, whether political, religious or philosophical; their interrelatedness is communicated by the broad sweep of Wharton's fictional panorama and they can be seen as products of the historical conditions which form the background to Odo's story. The emblematic nature of the characterisation also acts as a means by which to clarify – for Wharton as artist – the complexities of the inheritance of her own North American civilisation. It was one of her primary, almost didactic, aims in the novel to spell out to her New World audience how essential it was for them to recognise the fact of social continuity, even of history itself, as America was about to enter the first century to which its own definitive history allowed it to lay full claim as shaper and mover of world events.

The mixture of philosophies and social allegiances which bring pressure to bear upon Odo do not generally impinge, except in matters of simple plot, upon his other main purpose in the novel which is also inextricably bound up with the American discovery of its rôle on the world stage – in this case, that of tourist. The attention paid to travelling and sight-seeing and the attendant effect upon the boundaries of the individual's expectations is, as elsewhere in Wharton, intimately connected with the development of the aesthetic sensibility and also with her special pedagogic intentions towards her American audience. Just as Madame de Staël has Corinne and Lord Nelvil conduct the reader on a guided tour of the Italian sights so Odo comes to Naples as a tourist. His journey from Monte Alloro is highly circuitous: he takes in several northern principalities, sets sail for Naples from Genoa – having once reflected upon the spiritual and architectural properties of that city – and after Naples moves on to Rome for further immersion in the past.

Odo's early, if untutored, exposure to devotional and classical painting prepares him for the Grand Tour of the principal Italian cities and their art treasures which is made expedient by his tacit banishment from Pianura, and the tour reaches its climax in his participation in an archaeological dig in Naples. This depiction of the literal excavation of the past is the most direct address in the text to a North American audience uneducated in the lessons of the past. Odo's archaeological adventures, in the company of 'a party of gentlemen in the saloon of Sir William Hamilton's famous villa of Posilipo',[19] provide direct and literal access to the foundations of civilisation, the 'famous' being offered as a tribute to the referential powers of the guidebook-trained reader. As rendered through the artefacts of the past by Odo, however, the lessons are redeemed from the limitations of the museum by the equalising emphasis of Wharton's prose upon both historic continuity and the organic: '. . . in his hands the rarest specimens of that buried art which, like some belated golden harvest, was now everywhere thrusting itself through the Neapolitan soil'.[20] In the use of the imagery of plant growth Wharton weighs the implications of the 'discovery' of the past, focusing on a development which is new and vital despite its concern with the ancient or neglected. The response of the individual – whether archaeologist or tourist – is what endows life.

The offering up of the Italian landscape as being perpetually in renewal through art and nature is made much of in both *The Valley of Decision* and in *Italian Backgrounds* where the linguistic emphasis falls upon the importance of the personal view:

The ancient Latin landscape, so time-furrowed and passion-scarred, lies virgin to the eye, fresh-bathed in floods of limpid air. The scene seems recreated by the imagination, it wears the pristine sparkle of those *Towers of fable immortal fashioned from mortal dreams* which lie beyond the geographer's boundaries, like the Oceanus of the early charts. . . .[21]

With 'virgin', 'fresh-bathed' and 'pristine' we are left in no doubt that Wharton is endeavouring to communicate to her audience the idea that there is a perspective which can be brought to bear on the Italian scene which need not be bound by a sense of the 'time-furrowed'; she translates Europe with the language of American possibility. At the end of the notes for the fragmentary 'Italy Again' she quotes Goethe's reaction to the spectacle of Rome: '"Was einer ist" – it all comes back to that'; the European past can be communicated by the guidebook, wherein its most obvious treasures are displayed, but it is only the traveller prepared to venture upon an independent view, make an independent judgement, who can discern the importance of the Italian background. In the novel and in the guidebooks, particularly *Italian Backgrounds*, the prelapsarian expectations of life in the New World are refracted back upon the Old. Odo is the first of Wharton's fictional explorers of the dreams beyond a specific geography and, in her description of his awakening to 'the great inheritance of the past',[22] the only non-American.

In going outside her own geography at the beginning of her writing career Wharton was able to chart a number of significant personal landmarks. Within the eighteenth-century Italian framework she could create a strong woman, Fulvia Vivaldi, although, unlike the women in the novels which Wharton sets in the contemporary world who are at the centre of her artistic concern, Fulvia has to be, in the end, subordinated to the larger historical purpose of the narrative. She could also lay the groundwork for an exploration of what she felt to be a personal and national aesthetic crisis, that of imitation. She describes, in the novel, the 'Princes and Cardinals' who are interested only in those artists who can be trusted to reproduce exactly the artefacts which reflect the system under which the men of wealth and influence have come to operate the power of patronage, rather than those who would use the past as a foundation upon which to build artistic change. Wharton separates the act of homage which also leaves room for change and the act of pure imitation – 'a sterile restoration of the letter'[23] – in much the same way as she distinguishes between those historical novelists who are without the 'visualizing gift' and those who can make history live again through their boldness with the material of the past. She wished to place herself within a tradition but a tradition which she could use as part of a process rather than as an end in itself. Additionally she could establish the affinities which she sought to communicate between herself, as American artist – belonging to a society which could only tolerate 'literature' if practised by such as Washington Irvine 'because, in spite of the disturbing fact that he "wrote" he was a gentleman'[24] – and her European counterparts through the

referential nature of her writing in the Italian novel. This facet of
her work can, however, be illuminated by a comparison with Sir
Walter Scott since Wharton's American situation at the turn of the
century actually bears close resemblance to the cultural conditions
of Scott's beginnings in the historical novel.

In his Chapter Seventy-Second or 'Postscript which should have
been a Preface' to *Waverley* Scott speaks of the changes which have
occurred in Scotland, changes of an order so dramatic that it has
become vital for him to commemorate the past before it becomes
unattainable:

> There is no European nation which, within the course of half a
> century, or little more, has undergone so complete a change as
> this kingdom of Scotland. . . . The gradual influx of wealth, and
> extension of commerce, have since united to render the present
> people of Scotland a class of beings as different from their
> grandfathers as the existing English are from those of Queen
> Elizabeth's time.[25]

The cadence of Scott's remarks is echoed, over one hundred years
later, by Wharton when explaining the authorial motivation to
record the past in her final autobiography, *A Backward Glance*:

> The first change came in the [1880s] with the earliest detachment
> of big money-makers from the West, soon to be followed by the
> Lords of Pittsburgh. . . . what had seemed unalterable rules of
> conduct became of a sudden observances as quaintly arbitrary as
> the domestic rites of the Pharoahs. Between the point of view of
> my Huguenot great-great-grandfather, who came from the
> French Palatinate to participate in the founding of New Rochelle,
> and my own father, who died in 1882, there were fewer
> differences than between my father and the post-war generation
> of Americans.[26]

Like Scott, Wharton states the need, as she sees it, to memorialise
the past before it recedes from her grasp. The primary movers of
change in the view of both authors, despite a century's difference
between the date of their writing, are the upwardly mobile
manufacturing classes. A point in the distant past – whether
Elizabethan England or the settlement of New Rochelle – is
invoked as a simple point of contrast to the present day in order to

emphasise the recent rapidity of social and economic change, both writers having been creatively inspired by a powerful sense of dislocation.

Wharton's historical novels, *The Valley of Decision*, *The Age of Innocence*, (1920), and *The Buccaneers*, (1938), are all concerned, like Scott in *Waverley*, with the prior civilisation, not the instruments of change. The new money finds its way into the novels which Wharton sets in the contemporary world – *The House of Mirth* in 1905 and *The Custom of the Country* in 1913 for example – but the volumes which mark the beginning, middle and end of her writing career are all retrievals of the past. In many ways, especially when considering the closeness of the structural principles of the historical novel to those of autobiography, *The Age of Innocence* and *The Buccaneers* relate closely to the repeated attempts by Wharton to memorialise her own life, to impose an order on the past via the printed page. *The Valley of Decision*, however, simply by choice and location of subject, is revealing of the wider concerns in art and history with which she began her career as a novelist, as well as her need to locate the personal, the American, present in the European past. For Wharton, the history of Italy is also the history of the United States. The sense of relatedness which is built into the successful historical novel and which Georg Lukács describes as 'the prehistory of the present'[27] – in this case the foundations and background of an American present – is as much evident in eighteenth-century Italy as in 'the founding of New Rochelle'. The lessons to be learned from the exploration of similarities between the society portrayed in *The Valley of Decision* and the cultural conditions of turn-of-the-century America are important considerations in Wharton's treatment of the historical subject, but the eighteenth-century Italy of which she wrote is more than an historical model, it is also an aesthetic and moral model. Wharton's choice of subject reveals her powerful and enduring

reverence for the accumulated experiences of the past, readiness to puzzle out their meaning, unwillingness to disturb rashly results so powerfully willed, so laboriously arrived at – the desire, in short, to keep intact as many links as possible between yesterday and tomorrow, to lose, in the ardour of new experiment, the least that may be of the long rich heritage of human experience.[28]

– such being the inspiration for much of her writing, not least her non-fiction where her didactic motivation could be more straight-forwardly enacted than in the novel.

Wharton's first travel or guidebook, *Italian Villas and Their Gardens*, published in 1904, developed out of a commission from the *Century* to write a series of articles on the subject to appear in the magazine in 1903. As R. W. B. Lewis points out in his bio-graphy, *Edith Wharton*, a precedent had been set in this line by the same magazine when they commissioned W. D. Howells to write on Tuscan cities in the 1880s. Wharton's qualifications for the task, for the magazine's purposes, were her two published texts: *The Valley of Decision* and her first book, *The Decoration of Houses*, a treatise on exterior and interior design and taste, co-written with the architect, Ogden Codman Jnr. and published in 1897. The novel showed the artist inspired by the Italian scene and the non-fiction displayed her professional and practical competence to good effect. The combination of qualities which appealed to the editor of the *Century* is worth noting very precisely, however, as it is actually the foundation upon which all Wharton's writing is built, both in fiction and non-fiction. The tension generated by her urge to defend the natural artist and the 'intelligent amateur' and her admiration for the results of 'systematized study' is a positive one, providing a constant source of energy for her work. This internal debate receives its first real airing in these early works where she makes a distinction between two different modes of apprehension, here in *Italian Backgrounds*:

> But these are among the catalogued riches of the city. The guidebooks point to them, they lie in the beaten track of sight-seeing, and it is rather in the intervals between such systematized study of the past, in the parentheses of travel, that one obtains those more intimate glimpses which help to com-pose the image of each city, to preserve its personality in the traveller's mind.[29]

She chooses to express the individual, reflective response to travel in a metaphor of written composition – as the 'parentheses' of the guidebook experience – so as to illustrate the relationship between the two: the first, the informed, surrounds and supports the second, the felt.

In *Italian Villas and Their Gardens* Wharton combines the voice of the scholar, the tourist and the pedagogue in a generally happy and always informative blend. She writes of abstract principles of design but illustrates her argument with many examples of villas all over the country and with biographical details of the garden architects responsible for them. The book is chiefly concerned, as its title suggests, with the relationship, the balance, between the interior and the exterior design of the Italian villa and also the manner in which the house complements and is complemented by the garden. She sees the development of garden art in Italy in parallel with the larger processes of social change, 'the rapid flowering of Italian civilization';[30] her appreciation of the villas and their gardens being the means by which to convey her admiration for the whole-cultural nature of the Italian aesthetic, that is, the desire to make 'a garden as well adapted to its surroundings as were the models which inspired it'. This aesthetic, a topographical aesthetic, is not only given as a description but as a warning to her audience – defined early in the text as North American – against easy borrowing, against acquisitive tourism: 'what can I bring away from here? ... Not this or that amputated statue, or broken bas-relief, or fragmentary effect of any sort, but a sense of the informing spirit – an understanding of the gardener's purpose, and of the uses to which he meant his garden to be put'.[31] Understanding of intent is all, any thoughtless procurement of the souvenir is destructive – 'amputated', 'broken', 'fragmentary', – whereas a notion of the 'informing spirit' is always transferable to one's own landscape.

It is in *Italian Backgrounds*, a more general but also more personal series of travel sketches, however, that Wharton expounds most clearly her own inspiration and methodology as writer of guide-books in a manner which can, as already noted in discussion of *The Valley of Decision*, be taken to apply to the whole range of her artistic output:

As with the study of Italian pictures, so it is with Italy herself. The country is divided, not in *partes tres*, but in two: a foreground and a background. The foreground is the property of the guide-book and of its product, the mechanical sight-seer; the background, that of the dawdler, the dreamer and the serious student of Italy. This distinction does not imply any depreciation of the foreground. It must be known thoroughly before the middle distance can be enjoyed; there is no short cut to an intimacy with Italy.[32]

The 'foreground', the province of the guidebook, is seen to contain the museum pieces to which there is a set, learned response. This is not to say, however, that in order to avoid classification as a mechanised 'sight-seer' one's approach as a tourist must be divorced from 'tradition', only 'detached'. The conventions she discusses are those of the outsider trained in the skill of studying the alien culture through the representative artefact, and, for the American audience she assumes, this museum-trained mode of apprehension is perhaps all that is possible at first. This initial response, however, is actually indispensable to a later, fuller understanding, the 'mechanical' must come before 'intimacy' can be achieved. From the guidebook initiation – which Wharton herself, as she explains in the unpublished autobiographical fragment 'Life and I', found so valuable as a nineteen-year-old untutored tourist in Italy: 'I cannot disown my debt to Ruskin. To Florence and Venice his little volumes gave a meaning, a sense of organic relation, which no other books attainable for me at that time could possibly have conveyed'[33] – it is then possible to move onto an independent view. It was such an independent view which had led her personally, against expert advice, to the discovery of the mis-dating and consequent neglect of some terra-cotta statues of the Passion in the monastery of San Vivaldo, 'the rare sensation of an artistic discovery made in the heart of the most carefully-explored artistic hunting-ground of Europe',[34] in the chapter 'A Tuscan Shrine' which forms the centre-piece of *Italian Backgrounds*.

To achieve such confidence in one's own instincts, one's own vision, a much larger overview of the subject is vital; it must take into account the whole life of the country and its people and express the coherence of the relationship between the art, architecture and the landscape: 'It is because Italian art so interpenetrated Italian life, because the humblest stone-mason followed in some sort the lines of the great architects, and the modeller of village Madonnas the composition of the great sculptors, that the monumental foreground and the unregarded distances behind it so continually interpret and expound each other'.[35] It is this interrelatedness which actually underpins Wharton's own aesthetic. Her writing is various in its effects, its location and, often, its style, but it is unfailingly 'As well adapted to its surroundings as the models which inspired it' whether those models were to be found in another civilisation, like France or Italy, in a particular genre, like the historical novel or the autobiography, or in her own city, in 'the material nearest to hand, and most familiarly my own'[36] in *The House of Mirth*, the next novel she wrote and the text which shows Wharton exercising the most precise topographical control of her material.

2

The Customs of the Country: France

As discussed in the Introduction to this study the novels and travel guides in which Wharton concerns herself with the civilisation of France mark a period of transition in her writing. These works chart a movement from the Europe which she sought to illuminate for her American audience in *The Valley of Decision* to a Europe made familiar to her compatriots through the experiences of both war and tourism; the European scene no longer needed to be explicated in the same way. From the Napoleonic War which ends *The Valley of Decision* to the publication of her novel, *A Son at the Front*, five years after the end of the first world war, the progress of Wharton's work reflects a larger cultural passage from the Europe which had been, in the words of Nathaniel Hawthorne, a locus for 'romance', towards a world where American 'actualities'[1] would now dominate. As Wharton expressed it in an essay 'The Great American Novel', published in the *Yale Review* in 1927. 'We [Americans] have, in fact, internationalized the earth, to the deep detriment of its picturesqueness'.[2]

Treating her French works as a homogeneous group also, however, provides an opportunity to nail a canard about the life and works of Edith Wharton: the traditional critical view that she was but a pale imitator of Henry James in her style and subject matter. Perhaps the main reason why she has not been taken seriously as an artist until recently is the mistaken attribution to her of Jamesian intentions and ambitions and nothing did more to propagate that view than the malicious undermining of her work by Percy Lubbock, that most slavish of Jamesians, in his biography of her, published in 1947, ten years after her death.[3]

Wharton and James were great friends and she did owe to him an enormous debt in terms of that friendship and also, undeniably, as an artist; here, I hope to indicate the extent of that debt and to illuminate both the positive and negative aspects of James's influence. Aside from the fact that their subjects often overlapped, as was inevitable when their similar backgrounds and expatriate lifestyles are considered, there is only one instance, in the novel *The Reef*, published in 1912, where Wharton loses her own voice and finds that of James. Both the language and the treatment of the subject are an act of deference to him and he lavished praise on the novel in recognition of this in a letter written to her after its publication: 'the finest thing you have done; both *more* done than even the best of your other doing and more worth it through intrinsic value, interest and beauty'.[4] The nature of this 'doing' actually causes Wharton to be un'done', at least temporarily, and it is only when she moves back into her own voice, with the novel *The Custom of the Country* – incurring James's disapproval in the process – that she is able to achieve true authorial independence in the synthesis of her idea of France with an American narrative.

The first work of fiction which Wharton set in France, her novella, *Madame de Treymes*, uses the work of its distinguished ancestors, most notably Henry James's novel, *The American*, in the same way as the principal French family of the story, the Malrives, use theirs: for purposes of both continuity and display. The action of the novella takes place entirely in Paris; people leave the city only if it is politic for them to absent themselves for a period or if they have fallen into public disgrace, and we re-encounter them only when they are once more in the capital. The hero of the piece, John Durham, is in the act of proposing marriage to Fanny de Malrive, formerly Fanny Frisbee of New York, whose marriage to a Frenchman of long pedigree and little patience has ended unsuccessfully in separation. It is made plain by Wharton that John Durham had many opportunities in their mutual New York past to propose marriage to the then unmarried Fanny, but, as she has him acknowledge to himself:

> there were, with minor modifications, many other Fanny Frisbees; whereas never before, within his ken, had there been a Fanny de Malrive.... She was the same, but so mysteriously changed! And it was the mystery, the sense of unprobed depths of initiation, which drew him to her as her freshness had never drawn him.[5]

It is in the drawing of the desirability of a Fanny de Malrive over a Fanny Frisbee that Wharton's attention is engaged. She concentrates on the way in which Fanny has been enriched and matured by her exposure to 'the whole width of the civilization into which her marriage had absorbed her'.[6] There is a coherence in Fanny's actions and a certainty in her expectations within French society which provide her with a firm basis upon which to proceed even if a part of that firmness is in knowing the strict limits to which one must adhere. If Fanny has fallen from innocence, from 'freshness' to 'initiation', then in that fall there inheres a cultural value which 'lends point and perspective to the slightest contact between the sexes'[7] and makes the woman influential and powerful.

Wharton highlights the superficial irony of the fact that in the society where the most constraints would seem to operate, where even John Durham's innocent stroll with Fanny de Malrive is 'fraught with unspecified possibilities',[8] the possibilities for the female are actually greatest. It is the female exclusion from significant American life that Wharton is dealing with in all her 'French' books and the limitations of a culture which wastes half of its human resources are always implicit in the text. In *The Custom of the Country*, the culmination of her work in this vein, Charles Bowen, the cross-cultural mediator so often found in Wharton novels, formulates the reason for the social divergences between continents, locating as the key distinction the difference in attitude to women:

> Why does the European woman interest herself so much more in what the men are doing? Because she's so important to them that they make it worth her while! She's not a parenthesis, as she is here – she's in the very middle of the picture. I'm not implying that Ralph isn't interested in his wife – he's a passionate, a pathetic exception. But even he has to conform to an environment where all the romantic values are reversed. Where does the real life of most American men lie? In some woman's drawing-room or in their offices? The answer's obvious, isn't it? The emotional centre of gravity's not the same in the two hemispheres. In the effete societies it's love, in our new one it's business. In America the real *crime passionnel* is a 'big steal' – there's more excitement in wrecking railways than homes.[9]

Wharton's carefully mixed metaphor mixes also forms of art and whilst women are enclosed by both, bracketed or framed, the textual metaphor describes her as something expressed in a segregated language whilst the visual art comparison contains at least the possibility of a central rôle. Bowen describes European societies as 'effete' and acknowledges, as does Fanny de Malrive before him, the likelihood of damage being done to the individual by the very defined nature of the social procedures which enclose them. However, when he talks of 'love' he means the notion, which Wharton writes of again and again in *Madame de Treymes*, of real relationship – in love and friendship – between the sexes. In her book, *French Ways and Their Meaning*, published in 1919, Wharton says:

> In America ... woman, in the immense majority of cases, has roamed through life in absolute freedom of communion with young men until the day when the rounding out of her own experience by marriage puts her in a position to become a social influence; and from that day she is cut off from men's society in all but the most formal and intermittent ways. On her wedding-day she ceases, in any open, frank and recognised manner, to be an influence in the lives of the men of the community to which she belongs.
>
> ... the French have always recognised that, as a social factor, a woman does not count until she is married; and in the well-to-do classes girls marry extremely young, and the married woman has always had extraordinary social freedom. The famous French 'Salon', the best school of talk and ideas that the modern world has known, was based on the belief that the most stimulating conversation in the world is that between intelligent men and women who see each other often enough to be on terms of frank and easy friendship.[10]

It is the disenfranchisement of women by marriage that retards the development of a real civilisation in Wharton's view; the American removal of what Bowen calls 'business' from the 'drawing-room' means that women are never involved in the whole of life. Matters aesthetic and moral are left at home and are thereby marginalised; the constitutional separation of church and state effectively means the separation of family and business and there is no dialogue between the two. When Wharton writes 'The Frenchwoman rules French life, and she rules it under a triple crown, as a business woman, as a mother, and above all as an artist',[11] she is describing an integrated existence. Where the entire social structure contains rather than excludes the female then her influence is taken seriously. The Malrives have to stoop to trickery to try and regain possession of the young Marquis, but it is because Fanny has realised the extent of her power that they must do this; for them the only '*crime passionnel*' is one which is carried out for the family, even if this also means that it must be carried out within the family.

In her travel writing Wharton consistently puts forward a theory of American aesthetic deprivation which she contrasts with the rich variety and, above all, the humanised nature of the French landscape. She ironically presents the American tourist as being privileged by such deprivation, the commercial imperatives of architectural style in her own country forming an illuminating contrast to the experience of travel and sight-seeing in Europe:

> to come on this vigorous bit of mediaeval arrogance, with the little houses of Dourdan still ducking their humble roofs to it in an obsequious circle – well! to taste the full flavour of such sensations, it is worth while to be of a country where the last new grain-elevator or office building is the only monument that receives homage from the surrounding architecture.[12]

In the fiction Wharton takes this concept of cultural deprivation and converts it to the principle of renunciation: the American's sole resource in the face of European complexity is to preserve both simplicity and integrity in resignation. John Durham, like James's Christopher Newman of *The American* and Lambert Strether of *The Ambassadors*, must give up not only the woman he loves but also Paris itself and the opportunity to move beyond the city of the visitor towards a more sophisticated knowledge of France. In his introduction to *A Little Tour in France*, published in 1883, Henry James makes much of the fact that his compatriots, despite their characteristic tendency as tourists to prefer the country to the city, nevertheless reverse their normal predilections when in France and favour Paris at the expense of the rest of the country. In tune with the American traveller's preference both Wharton and James locate their fictions at the site of the commonest cultural confrontation, Paris, and in doing so imitate the general experience. As well as defining the cross-cultural encounter topographically, both authors also use the commonest of human processes, that of courtship and marriage, to place even more definitively the nature of the difference between native and tourist. Part of what is being renounced by John Durham and by his predecessors in James's fiction, is any pretence towards cultural coherence; all ultimately surrender to a complexity which manifests itself as a superior sense of place which in turn bestows a more highly developed sense of self. The action of *Madame de Treymes* never leaves the city because John Durham is never allowed to become a part of real French life; the priorities of the natives lie outside Paris and it is only when her Americans abroad understand this that Wharton shows them able to reach some sort of personal maturity and self-realisation.

At the heart of Wharton's writing in her French works, both fiction and non-fiction, is an idea of geographical specificity, a close identification between the individual and the dwelling place – either literally a house or a place in the sense of a rôle. An achieved sense of self and environment is the principle upon which Wharton leaves Paris to tour the countryside in *A Motor-Flight Through France*. As she says: 'here in northern France, . . . one understands the higher beauty of land developed, humanised, brought into relation to life and history, as compared with the raw material with which the greater part of our own hemisphere is still clothed'.[13] She then goes on to describe a literary pilgrimage which many had made before her, to the home of George Sand, Nohant, in terms of those topographic certainties which a house and its regional identity could bestow upon its occupier. Wharton sees Nohant as the repository of all the constants which made up Sand's entire social and moral world:

> an old house so marked in its very plainness, its conformity, must have exerted, over a mind as sensitive as hers, an unper- ceived but persistent influence, giving her that centralising weight of association and habit which is too often lacking in modern character, and standing ever before her as the shrine of those household pieties to which, inconsistently enough, but none the less genuinely, the devotion of her last years was paid.[14]

Nohant's 'plainness' and 'conformity' are posited as the vital counterparts to, or even the foundations of, the well-known – and here unspoken – irregularities in George Sand's lifestyle in much the same way as elsewhere Wharton puts forward the fact of George Eliot's unconventional life with G. H. Lewes as the crucial rationale for the scrupulously conventional morality of her novels. The dialogue between the two sides of the woman's life is fruitful, but it can only be so because of the specific rooting of self, or a part of the self, in a wider cultural certainty: Nohant for Sand, creative work for Eliot, vigorous motherhood for Wharton's Fanny de Malrive – all these ensure inclusion in a larger order and where there is inclusion there is also real consideration and respect.

The Reef, published in 1912, and the next novel by Wharton to be set in France, is also concerned with the removal of the American woman from her native land to Europe: Anna Leath, like Fanny de Malrive, has discovered the paradoxically liberating effects of social and geographical predictability. *The Reef* has its French background in common with *Madame de Treymes* but, whilst the foreground deals with those of Wharton's concerns which recur throughout the French texts, the style in which it is written sets up something of a diversion. The reader is re-routed through a number of James-derived linguistic delays and distractions in much the same way as the receptive traveller, sampling for the first time the touristic possibilities of the motor-car, is constantly diverted and ensnared by the richness of the French landscape in *A Motor-Flight Through France*:

> It is easy enough, glancing down the long page of the Guide Continental, to slip by such names as Versailles, Rambouillet, Chartres and Valençay, in one's dash for the objective point; but there is no slipping by them in the motor, they lurk there in one's path, throwing out great loops of persuasion, arresting one's flight, complicating one's impressions, oppressing, bewildering one with the renewed, half-forgotten sense of the hoarded richness of France.[15]

To attempt a dash for the objective point, however, the internal structure of character and event in *The Reef* displays the coherence of Wharton's textual strategy, in both the fiction and non-fiction, in topographical terms, and it is this which provides the real interest of the novel.

There are two main centres of action in the story, Paris, and the château, Givré, which is the home of the central protagonist, Anna Leath. These two locations extend and illuminate the consideration of difference between the attitudes of native and tourist to the capital city and the countryside touched on by James in *A Little*

Tour in France and taken up by Wharton in her writing. To examine the rôle of the provinces first, in the shape of the château, Givré, Wharton shows how the house makes Anna, its chief occupant, self-sufficient. She is geographically and emotionally settled, the description of her feelings toward the house charting her passage from youth to maturity:

> The possibilities which the place had then represented were still vividly present to her. The mere phrase 'a French château' had called up to her youthful fancy a throng of romantic associations, poetic, pictorial and emotional; and the serene face of the old house seated in its park among the poplar-bordered meadows of middle France had seemed, on her first sight of it, to hold out to her a fate as noble and dignified as its own mien. Though she could still call up that phase of feeling it had long since passed, and the house had become to her the very symbol of narrowness and monotony. Then, with the passing of years, it had gradually acquired a less inimical character, had become, not again a castle of dreams, evoker of fair images and romantic legend, but the shell of a life slowly adjusted to its dwelling: the place one came back to, the place where one had one's duties, one's habits and one's books, the place one would naturally live in till one died: a dull house, an inconvenient house, of which one knew all the defects, the shabbinesses, the discomforts, but to which one was so used that one could hardly, after so long a time, think oneself away from it without suffering a certain loss of identity.[16]

The three phases of Anna's relationship with Givré imitate the larger development in Wharton's expatriates' attitude to France and also her ideas about the benefits gradually but inevitably conferred by certainties of structure – either of the social organisation or the material fabric of a dwelling. Anna came to the house, as she came to Europe and to her marriage, with 'a throng of romantic associations' which, as she ceases to be a tourist – and open only to the most superficial of sensations – disperse, leaving her with a feeling of confinement. However, with the fading of illusion a sense of that which Wharton later, in *The Age of Innocence*, terms 'the dignity of a duty',[17] comes to inhabit the house alongside her. In language which recalls her description of George Sand's Nohant, Wharton conveys an idea of the sanctity which inheres in the expected; the house has become a centre of self because within it are located the certainties of so many lifetimes. The scene – and its human significance – is broadened out by a movement from the specific, the personal pronoun, to the generic; a sense of community, of shared experience, is established. Again, as with Fanny de Malrive's acknowledgement of the negative aspects of the Faubourg, the unpleasant qualities of the structure, 'the shabbinesses, the discomforts', are directly articulated but they are a signal part of mature recognition, a further revelation of control over, and real relationship with, one's environment. Anna passes beyond naïve tourism, the general American experience, because of her residence at Givré.

Anna Leath is counterbalanced in the novel by Sophy Viner, the itinerant governess/companion befriended by George Darrow, Anna's long-time suitor, in Paris. Sophy is apparently sophisticated; her life has put the 'hard stamp of experience'[18] upon her features but she brings only innocent expectations to Paris. It is her immaturity which Darrow, in fact, finds engaging, for as long, that is, as the affair and the good weather last. He sets a tone of cultural condescension in their relationship and in doing so flirts with a naïve view of the city which he has, in truth, long outgrown. Darrow has no real roots – Wharton making this feature of his character literal in his profession as a diplomat – and he is able to adjust his sense of self to the demands of the Parisian present whilst waiting to be summoned by Anna to another kind of life in the country:

> At the outset, he had felt no special sense of responsibility. He was satisfied that he had struck the right note, and convinced of his power of sustaining it. The whole incident had somehow seemed, in spite of its vulgar setting and its inevitable prosaic propinquities, to be enacting itself in some unmapped region outside the pale of the usual. It was not like anything that had ever happened to him before, or in which he had ever pictured himself as likely to be involved; but that, at first, had seemed no argument against his fitness to deal with it.
>
> Perhaps but for the three days' rain he might have got away without a doubt as to his adequacy. The rain had made all the difference. It had thrown the whole picture out of perspective, blotted out the mystery of the remoter planes and the enchantment of the middle distance, and thrust into prominence every commonplace fact of the foreground. It was the kind of situation

that was not helped by being thought over; and by the perversity of circumstance he had been forced into the unwilling contemplation of its every aspect. . . .[19]

The affair is defined, for Darrow, by its lack of relatedness to any topographical certainty; he invents both the time and the place, having undertaken to proceed without a guidebook. Wharton shows Darrow attempting to distance the experience with use of the language of visual art. He had never 'pictured' such a scene, but once having become involved he loses the power to step outside it – the power of the aesthete-tourist which he brought to the relationship – and the 'perspective' which he was first able to maintain on the affair is destroyed by the simple visual distortion of the rain.

The affair between Darrow and Sophy, forming the main part of Book One of *The Reef*, takes place in the capital city: their encounter mimics the touristic experience in Paris where the significance of what is seen is dependent upon the level of sophistication which the individual brings to the city. Both Darrow and Sophy are suspended from their present reality in their relation to Paris; for Darrow the experience is simultaneously an exercise in memory and an experiment, whilst for Sophy the city is a stage-setting, a 'drop-scene'[20] as Wharton terms it, before which she can play a central rôle entirely unrelated to her usual social insignificance, or indeed, her right to a geographical certainty. When Darrow comes to look back on the affair and other 'declines' he describes it as 'parenthetic':[21] the woman is again enclosed within the bounds of an excluded language. His act of memory, before he encounters her again at Givré, expels her from the centre of the scene. Both Sophy and Darrow go to the country, however, when they turn to the business which brought them to France; for Sophy the need to gain employment forces her to leave Paris, and when Darrow resumes his courtship of Anna, he must go to Givré. As they leave tourism and the temporary behind them so they, and Wharton's expatriates in general, follow the pattern set for them by the French; the general desire is, as Ford Madox Ford describes it in his 1926 book, *A Mirror to France*, for the natives, 'to get back to their pays'.[22] *The Reef* moves from city to country, the structure of the novel imitating the nature of the experience; the episodic and thematic construction of all Wharton's French work parallels the movement of the American abroad towards integration or, in some cases, alienation.

In her endeavour to convey a sense of the 'richness and multiplicity'[23] of the French scene and, indeed, the general human scene in this novel, Wharton, as I have already suggested, seeks refuge in or defers to a Jamesian stylistic precedent. Whether or not *The Reef* was a deliberate exercise in the Jamesian mode its relative failure as a novel really inheres in Wharton's use of the limited point of view. There is something too professional in the way in which she tells her story here: the language is self-conscious, the use of adjectives excessive and there is too much reliance upon stretches of narrated significance – she tells us too often that she is engaged upon 'the evocation of great perspectives of feeling'.[24] Wharton is most successful when she locates her characters within those terms of reference which inform the travel books, that is, through light and darkness and, of course, landscape. However, her ideas are generally stronger than her expression in *The Reef* because she lets herself be diverted by the indirect, by methods which are off the point; in fact, by the same kind of distractions which she talked about encountering on the route from Paris to Poitiers even though, in reading the guidebook, she could believe that she had them under control. The difference here, however, is that in the novel they are not directly acknowledged as diversions, as digressions into someone else's stylistic toils. It is as if the writing of the novel exemplifies that approach which Wharton criticises in *A Motor-Flight Through France* as the 'specialist'[25] mode of expression and appreciation.

To look in detail at one section of the text before returning to a discussion of Wharton's main thematic concerns, however, will illustrate the derivative nature of some of the writing – here Sophy explains her background to Darrow:

> The impecunious compatriots had found Mrs. Murret for her, and it was partly on their account (because they were such dears, and so unconscious, poor confiding things, of what they were letting her in for) that Sophy had stuck it out so long in the dreadful house in Chelsea. The Farlows, she explained to Darrow, were the best friends she had ever had (and the only ones who had ever 'been decent' about Laura, whom they had seen once, and intensely admired); but even after twenty years

of Paris they were the most incorrigibly inexperienced angels, and quite persuaded that Mrs. Murret was a woman of great intellectual eminence, and the house at Chelsea 'the last of the *salons*' – Darrow knew what she meant? And she hadn't liked to undeceive them, knowing that to do so would be virtually to throw herself back on their hands, and feeling, moreover, after her previous experiences, the urgent need of gaining, at any cost, a name for stability; besides which – she threw it off with a slight laugh – no other chance, in all these years, had happened to come to her.[26]

The use of the parenthetic, the hesitancies of the syntax and decoration of the infinitives, instead of illuminating the farther reaches of Sophy's past life simply slow down recognition of the arbitrary nature of the influences and events which have shaped her; Sophy herself is curiously absent from the text. Wharton here, in her choice of language and sentence structure, has endowed the writing with a fixed quality which belies the randomness of the experience described. Although the retrospective cast of the narrative inevitably means that a rationale of sequence and form will be imposed upon the events of the past, the constant use of qualifying phrases serves only to exclude Sophy from participation in her own history. In echoing the guarded manner in which James's characters communicate and are communicated Wharton has fallen into the trap against which she perpetually warns her reader/traveller: the belief that imitation of the professional or precedential voice of the guidebook is a substitute for feeling. All the significance of the past, all its emotion, is here compressed – often literally in parenthesis – and denied; the language is ultimately lifeless.

Where Wharton is entirely successful in *The Reef*, however, is in her portrait of Anna Leath and in the contiguous depiction of the forms of innocence and experience. Wharton's creative treatment of these most traditional of American concerns makes valuable that surrender of naïvety which is more usually portrayed in negative terms. Commentators like Millicent Bell in her *Edith Wharton and Henry James* see Anna as the typical American ingénue: 'The Reef probes the "innocence" – symbolically American – of Anna Leath, and contrasts it with the "experience" of Sophy Viner, who is after the fall, has tasted of the apple . . .'.[27] Wharton makes it plain, however, that more than the occasional sexual adventure or a powdered cheek is required to make a truly experienced woman. Her structuring of innocence and experience in whole-cultural terms actually posits a maturity of self and social knowledge – associated elsewhere in American fiction with decadence or corruption in women – as the desired end. The awareness of matters emotional and carnal which Anna attains as a result of her initiation into the secrets of Sophy and Darrow's shared past is converted, in combination with the achieved sense of self which is hers at Givré, to something more tolerant, a human as well as a cultural maturity. It is the acknowledgement of Darrow's fault which enables Anna finally to accept him and, whilst Wharton is not explicit about the outcome of events, enough clues are dropped:

> She knew now that she could never give him up.[28]

> when he had given her the chance to free herself, everything had vanished from her mind but the blind fear of losing him; and she saw that he and she were as profoundly and inextricably bound together as two trees with interwoven roots.[29]

Anna makes finding Sophy the condition upon which she will be bound to give Darrow up; she tells herself that having once announced to Sophy that they are finished she will have to keep her word. However, before Anna can reach her, Sophy is once again absorbed into that world which exists without a specific geography – Mrs Murret's 'salon' – and Anna is left without the power of renunciation which is the last resort of the innocent. She is forced to assume active responsibility for her own life and to admit her knowledge of the circumstances, past and present, which invariably surround the conditions of choice.

The Reef discovers the individual reaction which is made substantial and illumined by the collective, human response and in returning again to Wharton's treatise, *French Ways and Their Meaning*, it can be seen that Wharton locates the reasons for the immaturity of the American woman in her sexual isolation:

> The reason why American women are not really 'grown up' in comparison with the women of the most highly civilised countries – such as France – is that all their semblance of freedom, activity and authority bears not much more likeness to real living

than the exercises of the Montessori infant. Real living, in any but the most elementary sense of the word, is a deep and complex and slowly-developed thing, the outcome of an old and rich social experience. It cannot be 'got-up' like gymnastics, or a proficiency in foreign languages; it has its roots in the fundamental things, and above all in close and constant and interesting and important relations between men and women.[30]

Anna Leath attains to a sense of real relationship with her world through her understanding and acceptance of the experience of others, as represented by both Givré and Darrow. In her next novel, *The Custom of the Country*, Wharton's writing is still consistent in being guided by the informing spirit of the French model. As her intention is to show that model wholly unregarded by the new breed of American traveller, however, its force is now almost entirely ironic.

Edith Wharton's movement into what Henry James in his 1914 essay, 'The New Novel', termed the 'satiric light',[31] in *The Custom of the Country*, is also her movement into the twentieth century. The central protagonist, Wharton's most magnificent creation, Undine Spragg, is unprecedented; not only does Undine herself operate without a sense of the past – American or European – but Wharton herself moves decisively away from the Jamesian model with which she experimented in *The Reef*. The form which she describes in her autobiography, *A Backward Glance*, as the 'chronicle-novel' and which she opposes to the novel – by implication *The Reef* – which contains 'the elaborate working out on all sides of a central situation,' is the proper medium for *The Custom of the Country*: 'I was chronicling the career of a particular young woman, and . . . to whatever hemisphere her fortunes carried her, my task was to record her ravages and pass on to her next phase'.[32]

Undine Spragg is held in the full glare of that 'satiric light' which James pinpointed as the 'only one in which the elements engaged could at all be focussed together'.[33] She is 'bathed in the bright publicity of the American air'[34] and as such represents the stripping down of civilisation to its most obvious features. Behind *The Custom of the Country*, however, in subdued tones and shades of possibility, is the text of *French Ways and Their Meaning*. All the points of reference towards which the novel motions us are formulated within the later book and nowhere is this more crucial than in the characterisation of Undine and her factitious place at the centre of the story. She sustains such a position only because she flouts the demands of anything but the relentless pursuit of 'experiments in happiness';[35] business, motherhood, art – all are as irrelevant as the act of marriage which she continually considers, and indeed carries out, but can never commit herself to. She is a modern version of the water-nymph who could only gain a soul by marrying a mortal; Undine marries mortals enough but never commits herself to the act and so remains soul-less. She has no idea of obligation or collective responsibility and so retains her inviolate status. Such an innocence derives from the exclusion of the American woman from the business of real life and in this manner has the New World version of the unfallen state been perverted. The Frenchwoman, as Wharton says, 'rules' on a principle of engagement with others – 'it is only the married woman who counts as a social factor'[36] – but Undine is the 'monstrously perfect result of the system';[37] where the system fails to accommodate the married woman as a social force and also fails to provide any other rôle for her to play or goal for her to aim at.

Wharton shows two American worlds in *The Custom of the Country*: the dying society of Ralph Marvell, the 'Reservation'[38] as he terms it, between which and the Faubourg of Raymond de Chelles, Charles Bowen can modulate without difficulty, and the new America, that being created by the 'Invaders' from the west. Undine's family are 'unlocalized'; they lodge in a series of hotels 'disconnected from any fixed habits';[39] with an 'obvious lack of any sense of relative values'[40] except those which Undine apportions to changing and moving targets from week to week. The new Americans are not without a sense of precedence, but this sense extends only so far as imitation, not comprehension. From the 'Looey' suites where the Spraggs restlessly perch at the beginning of the novel, to the society which the Americans abroad create for themselves in Paris, all is superficial, homage is paid to tradition in appearance only:

The dining-room of the Nouveau-Luxe represented, on such a spring evening, what unbounded material power had devised for the delusion of its leisure: a phantom 'society', with all the rules, smirks, gestures of its model, but evoked out of promiscuity and incoherence while the other had been the product of continuity and choice. And the instinct which had driven a new class of world-compellers to bind themselves to slavish imitations of the superseded, and their prompt and reverent faith in the reality of the sham they had created, seemed to Bowen the most satisfying proof of human permanence.[41]

Wharton is here detailing the failure, the superannuation, of the American gesture of integrity, of discretion, of the reflex of renunciation; there is no longer the same moral imperative towards maintaining a sense of independence between continents. An orgy of unconstrained 'imitation' is the inevitable result of the doctrine of acquisition and display. Undine, in an ironic echo of James's 1881 heroine, Isabel Archer, has laid claim to 'everything'.[42] She cannot, however, separate the material from the emotional and the value of the coveted object or subject is invariably destroyed in the possession.

Charles Bowen's anthropological eye, whilst illuminating the scene, also betrays the passiveness, the impotence of old New York in the face of the new 'world-compellers'. Bowen's New York *milieu* is Ralph Marvell's 'Reservation'; this particular America is a museum-piece because it has failed to impress upon its public any enduring sense of the 'root principles of conduct, social and political'[43] which have shaped it. Old New York is characterised by the subdued atmosphere of Laura Fairford's drawing-room and its murmured, exclusive, conversational style, new society by the noisy public display of the patrons of the dining-room of the Nouveau-Luxe. It is Raymond de Chelles, Undine's third husband, who defines the social scene which the new Americans carry all over the world with them, without regard to their precise location, as 'a kind of superior Bohemia, where one may be respectable without being bored'.[44] This sums up Undine's one ambition, although her desire to be respectable does not derive from any idea of personal or collective morality but from the simple need to protect her public image. Her enormous and uninstructed energy has no outlet in business or even in the cultural pursuits and 'good works' with which the women of Laura Fairford's background occupy themselves. When describing Undine's behaviour as she seeks to complete her conquest of Peter Van Degan Wharton says: 'she left her hands in Van Degan's. So Mr. Spragg might have felt at the tensest hour of the Pure Water move'.[45] She has no other opportunity to exercise her considerable commercial talents. Marriage is debased by such as Undine, not because she is any different from generations of women who have married for money or family obligation or any number of other reasons which have nothing to do with romantic love, but because she accepts none of the responsibilities which must accompany it. The business practice of the twentieth century, the style of Elmer Moffat which takes the shortest route to the quickest profit, is translated by Undine into the realm of personal relations. The custom of the country is that for the woman the 'money and motors and clothes are simply the big bribe she's paid for keeping out of some man's way!'[46] and Undine, as in all things, takes the custom to its furthest, most inhuman, reaches: 'it was impossible for Undine to understand a social organization which did not regard the indulging of women as its first purpose'.[47]

The Custom of the Country, then, is ultimately concerned with the problems of the positive incorporation of the woman and the way in which she participates in and influences the whole culture. The non-fiction counterpart to the novel, *French Ways and Their Meaning*, has a literal part to play in any reading of the book; its formulation of the French social structure provides the 'other' towards which the inadequacies and failings of Undine's world point us, and, in some respects, direct her. When she first meets Raymond de Chelles, for example, her view of Paris undergoes a complete change. She sees the life of the inhabitants of the Faubourg as the desired end: 'a life that made her own seem as undistinguished as the social existence of the Mealey House. . . . Once more all the accepted values were reversed'.[48] Undine is trapped in dissatisfaction by the instability of her own grounds for exercising judgement. A half-recognition of another social world brings discontent but not the means to resolve it; marrying Raymond serves only to increase her confusion as she does not know how to use the opportunities presented to the French wife for becoming involved in the whole of life.

There is an abyss of incomprehension dividing the new America from the old and from Europe, and not even the most persistent arbiter of the divide – the transatlantic liner – here named by Wharton, with tongue in cheek, the 'Semantic',[49] can bridge it. Undine does not connect the cossetting and indulgence of the American woman in material ways with the irrelevance of her social and cultural situation: 'a woman's picture has got to be pleasing. Who wants it about if it isn't?'[50] But the gap in Undine's sensibility is the nameless and fathomless source of her restlessness and discontent and the reason for the misery she causes. The deterministic language of the novel goes some way, however, towards removing the responsibility for Undine's actions from the individual to the culture. The world where precedents are all, Ralph Marvell's 'aboriginal' Washington Square, goes down before Undine's assault on its most sacred places because it has been complacent about its own enduring value and has not sought to communicate an idea of the principles it is based upon to the new Americans. Old New York has failed to adapt, to make its practices felt by, and relevant to, a changing and moving nation and the 'Invaders' from the west are thus deprived of any sense of precedence. The reaction of Ralph Marvell when he learns that Undine was previously married to Elmer Moffat leaves him:

> face to face with the uselessness, the irrelevance of all the old attitudes of appropriation and defiance. He seemed to be stumbling about in his inherited prejudices like a modern man in medieval armour. . . . Moffat still sat at his desk, unmoved and apparently uncomprehending. 'He doesn't even know what I'm feeling,' flashed through Ralph; and the whole archaic structure of his rites and sanctions tumbled down about him.[51]

The disparity between the relative investment of self in the act of marriage by the two men is highlighted by the whole-cultural reverberations of the personal shock for Ralph. There is an absolute intellectual and emotional affinity between Ralph's feelings and the 'rites and sanctions' which have nurtured them. His decision to die for the values of his ancestors marks the extinction of the society which upheld them. Any sense of community, of precedence and of participation in the real life of a culture, is entirely missing from the self-absorption of such as Undine, and the conditions of the social life in France are therefore put forward by Wharton as the basis of a fulfilling and coherent alternative or model – one which includes and therefore values the woman.

Wharton makes for herself a pedagogic rôle in the exposition of those ideas on the civilisation of France which inform the novels discussed in this chapter. This deliberate proselytizing on behalf of that which she saw as a worthy and generous culture does not, however, detract from the aesthetic richness of her writing in the three works of fiction which I have discussed here. The subtlety of the alternative which she is positing in the fiction is lost, however, when she comes to write those of her books still rooted in the

French culture but taking as their chief concern the first world war. The collection of essays published in 1915 as *Fighting France From Dunquerque to Belfort*, and the novels *The Marne*, (1918) and *A Son at the Front*, (1923), have a message which, in the novels particularly, overwhelms the medium. They are, nevertheless, important in terms of Wharton's formulation of the new transatlantic relation. The experience of the American in the European war is vital in the creation of the new topography, the post-war world.

3
Fighting France

The first world war had two major effects on Wharton's writing, one immediate and short-lived, the other gradual but enduring. Her instant reaction to the conflict was entirely specific as she dealt directly with the war experience in two novels and a collection of essays. The second and more profound influence of the war, however, can only be judged in terms of the effect which it had on the view of the world she projected in both the fiction and non-fiction written after the conflict was over. *A Son at the Front* and *The Marne*, her war novels, concentrate centrally on the question of American involvement in the fighting, but they also give an indication of what is to come, showing the movement in Wharton's writing away from the study of isolated male-female relations towards a concern with the family, and, via the family, to the children who are growing up with the twentieth century. The novels which follow the publication of *A Son at the Front*, *The Mother's Recompense* (1925), *Twilight Sleep* (1927) and *The Children* (1928), all deal with the society which emerges after the war, a war which brought the European and American continents into a completely new relationship.

Wharton's personal involvement with the war was not only expressed through her writing, however, and from the very outbreak of hostilities she was active in every possible way in efforts to alleviate the sufferings attendant upon the war. She had arranged to spend the late summer of 1914 in England, having rented both a country and a London house from Mrs Humphrey Ward, but returned to Paris when it became apparent that the war was not going to be the ten days' wonder that some had predicted. She immediately threw herself into the business of refugee work, work which was to lead to the award of the highest honour within a French President's gift when in 1916 she became a Chevalier of the Legion of Honour.

Before leaving for England she had established a workroom making clothes for sale in the United States, and on her return she provided a nursery for the children of the seamstresses; she set up an organisation called the American Hostels for Refugees which undertook to accommodate, find work for, give medical treatment to and feed and clothe those refugees who were arriving, in desperate need, in Paris, having fled from the battle zones. During its first full year of operation – 1915 – Wharton's enterprise assisted 9330 refugees and she had raised more than $100000 with which to do it. A network of committees administered the various parts of the organisation in France and even more committees, established through her contacts in America, were responsible for fund-raising. She made regular trips to the various front lines, discovering the extent of the devastation for herself and keeping constantly up to date with the areas of most pressing need. She went to Belgium, from whence the vast majority of her refugees originated, and, at the request of the Belgian government, formed a separate body – The Children of Flanders Rescue Committee – to look after orphans of the war, accommodating great numbers at short notice and providing education as well as food, clothes and shelter.

Remarkably, in the midst of all this, she managed to produce the series of essays published together as *Fighting France From Dunquerque to Belfort*, the first volume in which the war is her central subject. Published in 1915 the book contains six pieces: one describes the atmosphere of Paris at the start of war, four tell of visits to various parts of the front line and the final essay is a general piece which describes 'The Tone of France'. The collection has a straightforward pedagogic purpose for an audience not yet directly involved in the conflict. The absence of America from anything but philanthropic participation was bitterly felt by Wharton and the majority of her war writing is directed particularly at those who sought to maintain America's neutral stance.

Fighting France contains some of Wharton's most moving accounts of human suffering as she describes the war-torn countryside and its bereft inhabitants. The two works of fiction which came out of the war, however, are not quite so successful in this respect: being largely belated in their educational intentions, the message overwhelms the fictional medium. *The Marne*, published in 1918, a blatant piece of propaganda advocating participation in the war, is wholly and unflinchingly written at the dilatory American nation. *A Son at the Front*, published in 1923, five years after the end of the war, is a drawn-out study of development and change in the attitude of an ex-patriate American to the conflict. He moves from appeasement to participation in the struggle, and is burdened with representing the developing conscience of the whole American nation.

Throughout these three texts Wharton emphasises the relatedness of France and America in terms of their most fundamental creeds and attitudes. This is substantially achieved – not surprisingly in the context of war – at the expense of Germany, and in her 1919 volume, *French Ways and Their Meaning*, she locates 'the essential difference' between the allies and their foe in their respective attitudes to freedom:

> The German does not care to be free as long as he is well fed, well amused and making money. The Frenchman, like the American, wants to be free first of all, and free anyhow – free even when he might be better off, materially, if he lived under a benevolent autocracy.[1]

This racial simplification – comprehensible in terms of the propagandist purposes of the time – is also, however, meant as a warning to America. Wharton believed that anti-historical thinking, where the material comfort of the present and adherence to isolationist politics cause people to deny the lessons of the past, was responsible for making America complacent and she uses the chief character of *A Son at the Front* to illustrate this:

> What was war – any war – but an old European disease, an ancestral blood-madness seizing on the first pretext to slake its frenzy? Campton reminded himself again that he was the son of free institutions, of a country in no way responsible for the centuries of sinister diplomacy which had brought Europe to ruin, and was now trying to drag down America.[2]

American attempts to deny the relatedness of the war to their own concerns are a part, for Wharton, of the same old fear of commitment, of admission of responsibility, which she portrays in the three earlier novels which are partly or wholly set in France. Campton seeks to distance the conflict from its modern – and therefore American – context by use of the word 'ancestral' and a conjuring of 'centuries of sinister diplomacy'. He thus separates his own country from Europe by a denial of that idea of shared history which Wharton communicated to her American audience in *The*

Valley of Decision. She conveys, by the use of empty rhetoric here – 'the son of free institutions' – the folly of believing that an individual person or country can live in a vacuum. Ever-vigilant in the defence of her idea of European and American community, Wharton shows, by juxtaposition of the two, that if Campton wants to lay claim to 'free institutions' he cannot then disclaim responsibility for the painful 'centuries' which produced them.

The concerns of Wharton's writing do not change in the texts which deal with the war but as she becomes more desperate to impress upon her audience – not merely for pedagogic purposes but with propagandic intent – the value of continuity, of community, the necessity to be vigilant in defence of freedom, so the work suffers an attendant lack of control. For this reason the most successful of her war writing is the book of essays, *Fighting France*, where she can be direct in the expression of her beliefs. The novels do not carry the reader towards an understanding of the French model, as do *Madame de Treymes*, *The Reef* and *The Custom of the Country*, through the underlying creative force of the writing, but bludgeon us with anti-appeasement sentiment thinly disguised as fiction. *Fighting France* is effective because Wharton's emphasis, as she witnesses the scenes of destruction, is simply and movingly focused upon the complete loss of continuity in French life: the war has dislocated people and things to such an extent that identity has been entirely erased. The evidence of the annihilation 'of the long murmur of human effort, the rhythm of oft-repeated tasks',[3] in the decimated villages she visits gives Wharton her most literal and conclusive argument for realising the sanctity of 'the thousand and one bits of the past that give meaning and continuity to the present'.[4] There is a nightmarish suspension of the most common knowledge in the areas that suffered the heaviest fighting and in the essay, 'In Argonne', Wharton describes the obliteration of history itself from the landscape:

> In this part of the country, which is one of many cross-roads, we began to have unexpected difficulty in finding our way, for the names and distances on the mile-stones have all been effaced, the sign-posts thrown down and the enamelled *plaques* on the houses at the entrance to the villages removed. One report has it that this precaution was taken by the inhabitants at the approach of the invading army, another that the Germans themselves demolished the sign-posts and plastered over the mile-stones in

order to paint on them misleading and encouraging distances.
The result is extremely bewildering, for, all the villages being
either in ruins or uninhabited, there is no one to question but the
soldiers one meets, and their answer is almost invariably: 'We
don't know – we don't belong here.' One is in luck if one comes
across a sentinel who knows the name of the village he is
guarding.[5]

The specific topography of countless communities has been destroyed, the effect being the same whether defence or destruction
was the motive, and nowhere is Wharton's endowment of sanctity
upon rootedness, upon relationship, more effectively corroborated
than in her descriptions of the suffering attendant upon their loss
in war. She returns again and again to the ruins, where her
descriptions are of objects freighted with emotional significance:
'The photographs on the walls, the twigs of withered box above the
crucifixes, the old wedding-dresses in brass-clamped trunks, the
bundles of letters laboriously written and painfully
deciphered . . .',[6] and not only do they speak of intimate human
relationship but also of the structures which support them, church
and family.

Just as Wharton's pre-war fiction shows the business of real life
taking place in the provinces, away from the city, so the site of the
most profound suffering in war is in the countryside. The provinces are affected first and last whilst with Paris lies the responsibility for maintaining the bravura of the nation, the task for which
it has been protected from the reality of the fighting even to the
extent that casualties are sent not to the city's well-equipped
hospitals but instead to those outside:

> The motives for this disposal of the wounded have been much
> speculated upon and variously explained: one of its results may
> have been in the maintaining in Paris of the extraordinary moral
> health which has given its tone to the whole country, and which
> is now sound and strong enough to face the sight of any misery.[7]

Paris must be, in war as in peace, the show-place, the tourist
attraction with its eye on the world.

A close identification between the landscape and its human
inhabitants is familiar in Wharton's writing, in her novels and
travel books, but nowhere is it emphasised to such a degree as in

her war-works where the effects of the conflict are tragically evident in both. The land which has been fought over, its heritage effaced in violent upheaval, is now rendered, as were the possibilities for the tourist in Italy, in vocabulary imported from the America of the pioneer. In the essay, 'In Lorraine and the Vosges', she writes of 'frontier towns'[8] and of the flower that grows on the battlefields 'as a symbol of conscious human energy coming back to replant and rebuild the wilderness . . .'.[9] Paris, the model city, is protected so that it can serve as an example for human repossession of the landscape just as Europe as a whole once served for those who sought to possess the New World. The importance of reclaiming this newly created 'wilderness' for 'the civilised world'[10] is Wharton's message in *Fighting France*. However, in a lecture which she gave to American soldiers and sailors, sometime in 1918, she chooses to emphasise those features of the humanised landscape which are worthy of their emulation: 'the things we might all have – the splendid solid walls along the rivers, the beautiful bridges, the perfect roads, the exquisitely kept public parks and gardens',[11] not the effect of the fighting on the countryside. In order to extend the interchange and, indeed, interchangeability, between the two nations, and with her American audience immediately before her, she speaks most directly as the American abroad. Much as she may share her personal pronouns with her listeners, her message is most definitely that of the expatriate, the direction of the speech taking the restitution of the pre-war relationship between the two countries, a relationship in which France is the senior partner, as its central theme.

The novels published before 1914 which have as their foundation the civilisation of France also have implicit in the writing the superiority of the French way. The opinions which she found her compatriots espousing in the early years of the war emphasised, conversely, American moral and social pre-eminence and emphasised it in such a way that Wharton found untenable. As I have already mentioned she was distressed by America's early reluctance to become involved in the fighting – although this did not prevent her from feeling that Henry James had gone too far when he decided to become a British citizen in the summer of 1915 – and in *The Marne* she lampoons the brightly superior tone of some of her compatriots:

They found New York – Mrs Belknap's New York – buzzing with

war charities, yet apparently unaware of the war. . . . 'It makes us so *happy* to help,' beaming young women declared with a kind of ghoulish glee, doing up parcels, planning war-tableaux and charity dances, rushing to 'propaganda' lectures given by handsome French officers, and keeping up a kind of continuous picnic on the ruins of civilization.[12]

The novella tells the story of Troy Belknap, a young American, child of peripatetic parents, to whom Wharton entrusts many of her most cherished tenets about France, from her ideas about the exemplary rôle of Paris ('He himself was not shocked by the seeming indifference of Paris: he thought the gay theatres, the crowded shops, the restaurants groaning with abundance, were all healthy signs of the nation's irrepressible vitality. But he understood that America's young zeal might well be chilled by the first contact with this careless exuberance, so close to the lines where young men like himself were dying by day . . .'.[13]) to her reverence for the history of her adopted country and its worldwide influence: 'Troy felt what a wonderful help it must be to have that long rich past in one's blood. Every stone that France had carved, every song she had sung, every new idea she had struck out, every beauty she had created in her thousand fruitful years, was a tie between her and her children. These things were more glorious than her battles, for it was because of them that all civilization was bound up in her, and that nothing that concerned her could concern her only'.[14] At the outbreak of war Troy is only fifteen but has a much more developed sense of what is at stake in the conflict than either his parents or the Americans they consort with in Paris, where they are briefly marooned in 1914. The story follows the Belknaps as they go back to America, details the predominant tone of society as it participates in the war effort but maintains a judicious distance from the actual fighting, and then returns to France as Troy volunteers for a Red Cross Unit. Troy then skirts around the battlefields as an ambulance driver until the end of the novella when he actually takes part in the battle of the Marne, is wounded but rescued by a ghostly figure whom he believes to be his tutor, killed in the first year of the war, but never far from his thoughts. The story is a simple one and allows Wharton to illustrate her argument on a number of fronts: as Troy grows so does American understanding; we are never left in any doubt that the civilisation of the whole world is at stake and that America's participation in the fighting is what is needed to bring it to maturity as a nation.

The novella, although entirely blatant in its purpose, is not simply a war-mongering diatribe because Wharton cannot but express her horror of the human cost of the fighting as well as its grim necessity:

> war. . . . It emptied towns of their inhabitants as it emptied veins of their blood: it killed houses and lands as well as men. Out there, a few miles beyond the sunny vineyards and the low hills, men were dying at that very moment by hundreds, by thousands – and their motionless young bodies must have the same unnatural look as these wan ruins, these gutted houses and sterile fields. . . . War meant Death, Death, Death – Death everywhere and to everything.[15]

Wharton's love of France is evident in every word she writes in *The Marne* and goes some way towards softening what would otherwise be not much more than a story written to a crude anti-appeasement formula. What is missing here is the ironic control which makes *The Custom of the Country* such a *tour de force*; the strength of her feelings prevents Wharton from exercising any such regulation of the text.

A Son at the Front, whilst continuing to treat those of Wharton's cross-cultural preoccupations which are heightened by the war, is nevertheless written in a much lower key than *The Marne*. The question of American involvement is still at the centre of the novel but where Troy Belknap is always representative of the kind of attitude that Wharton hoped would ultimately prevail, John Campton, an expatriate artist, has to be convinced that he has a part to play in the struggle by the course of events in the novel. The story concerns Campton's relationship with his son, George, who usually lives with his mother and her second husband in America, but is about to visit him in Paris at the beginning of the novel.

Campton's attitude to the conflict is wholly derived from his anxieties about George, who was born in France and is therefore liable to be called up regardless of American involvement, and as he moves toward an understanding of the fact that other people are entitled to a relationship with his son, notably his ex-wife and her husband, so he grows to comprehend that no-one can afford to remain aloof from the principles at stake in the war. As George arrives in Paris so Campton reflects with a dispassion bordering on the risible: 'just as that was about to assure his happiness, here was this horrible world-catastrophe threatening to fall across his path',[16] but as the story progresses so does his recognition of his personal commitment to the fight: 'If France went, western civilization went with her; and then all they had believed in and been guided by would perish'.[17]

A Son at the Front, not published until five years after the end of the war, is a reiteration in the form of fiction of the reluctance of America to commit itself to Europe; but the opposition of individual and community, America being represented by the first and Europe by the second, is actually more centrally focused here than in Wharton's previous writing. Campton, like his country, is gradually enlightened as to the true nature of his involvement in 'western civilization' and therefore in the war. His detachment, which he struggles to maintain for the sake of protecting George, is eventually converted to partisanship and this development is made literal by George's engagement with the war effort, from office work behind the lines, to active service at the front, onward, inexorably, to his death.

There is something more than allegory in the story, however, as Wharton endeavours again to communicate to her audience a larger sense of France: 'An Idea; that was what France, ever since she had existed, had always been in the story of civilization; a luminous point about which striving visions and purposes could rally ... to thinkers, artists, to all creators, she had always been a second country'.[18] She is seeking, in the heightened atmosphere of the war, to show that France is actually an aesthetic model in itself, one to live by and die for if necessary and at the end of the novel, still numbed by George's death, Campton is vouchsafed a vision of both the wholeness and generosity of that model as the first American troops march through Paris:

> Such a summer morning it was – and such a strange grave beauty had fallen on the place! He seemed to understand for the first time – he who had served Beauty all his days – how profoundly, at certain hours, it may become the symbol of things hoped for and things died for. All those stately spaces and raying distances, witnesses of so many memorable scenes, might have been called together just as the setting for this one event – the sight of a few brown battalions passing over them like a feeble trail of insects.[19]

In and through Campton Wharton expresses that which has inspired her work in the French subject, particularly in the war writing – an all-pervasive sense of the importance of continuity – and that the American soldier should feature as a part of that continuity is finally the aim of *A Son at the Front*. The Parisian scene embraces the 'brown battalions' and in so doing establishes the widest possible community of interest and of values: historical, social, political, aesthetic, all spheres of life are seen to be held in common between continents. There is a spirit of reconciliation at the end of the novel and even art and commerce – usually diametrically opposed in the formulation of the ruling spirit of Wharton's Americans – are united in the form of Mr Brant, George's step-father, and Campton collaborating in the erection of a memorial to their son. Campton is seen finally as a Whitman-esque figure, visiting the servicemen at their clubs, appearing 'to them a vague unidentified figure, merely "the old gentleman" who was friendly to them'.[20] Bereft of his own son he can turn to the soldiers and sailors of his country for 'the life-giving power of a reality embraced and accepted'[21] which is also, at the last, acknowledged as a foundation upon which to build anew his work as an artist.

At about the same time as Wharton was writing *A Son at the Front* she was working on a novel called 'Tradition'; she made a plan of the story and actually wrote seven chapters before abandoning it. 'Tradition' is set in France but is not concerned with the war; rather it reverts to the treatment of 'household pieties' in the manner of the peace-time French writing, particularly *The Reef*, and describes the Grayson family home at Valbonne as being synonymous with their lifestyle:

> La Sainte Campagne had a character which no modern house could have had time to acquire, a modest aloofness and self-sufficingness corresponding exactly with Christina's own tastes, and with her parents' traditions. Tradition! That had always been the Grayson keynote, the recurring motive in the harmony of their secluded yet not unfriendly lives; and no dwelling could have embodied tradition more pleasantly than the house which they had softened into liveableness without diminishing its austerity.[22]

All this is to be expected from Wharton, both in the fiction and non-fiction, and the certainties represented by such a dwelling-place are also made manifest in Valbonne at large where the various expatriate residents are 'busy being particular and exclusive and disapproving'[23] about anything which might challenge the status quo. All the members of this community are vigilant in defence of values which elsewhere in Wharton's writing are spoken of with approbation and even pedagogic intent and so it comes as a surprise when it is revealed that the strictness of the residents in maintaining their standards of taste and conduct is based not upon certainty but upon fear. The colony of expatriates is, in fact, a 'penal settlement' and, as Wharton explains in her novel plan, every single reactionary member of the community has been 'obliged to exile themselves for financial or moral reasons'.[24]

In this story, then, one of the watchwords of the Whartonian artistic and social canon – 'Tradition' – is perverted and abused by the inhabitants of Valbonne; the last resource of the American innocent – the renunciation of people and place – is now degraded by being used as a part of a falsehood. Exclusivity, it seems, when taken so far, is literally criminal and the novel was planned to end with the Graysons 'and their friends sitting about the bridge table, and exchanging the same edifying views about the deterioration of society, and the incredible laxity of conduct in fashionable society, and congratulating themselves on the fact that they at least have lived apart and kept up the old-fashioned traditions'.[25]

I have introduced 'Tradition' to this discussion because it demonstrates very neatly a point about Wharton's work which could, after the single-mindedly conservative writing of the war years, be overlooked or even discounted. She did not lament the passing of old customs and beliefs because she was afraid of change but rather because of the manner of their passing in war; as she writes in *The Marne*, one of France's strongest features is its adaptability: '[Paul Gantier] had shown Troy how France had always been alive in every fibre, and how her inexhaustible vitality had been perceptually nourished on criticism, analysis and dis-satisfaction. "Self-satisfaction is death," he had said; "France is the phoenix-country always rising from the ashes of her recognized mistakes"'.[26] The message of Wharton's very first novel – that imitation without development, without human involvement in the process of change and growth, can only be sterile – is taken further in 'Tradition'. Here the need or desire to remain outside the influence of the real world is entirely perverse and leads inevitably to corruption and misery. The story is set in a very particular kind of France, the holiday coast, but the moral is, as ever, universal.

The victims of the falsehood here are the children of the colony, particularly Christina Grayson, whose innocence is abused by her parents in a manner to become familiar in Wharton's 1920s novels. The children of the post-war world are deprived, in Wharton's terms, of the guidance of the past because it is either adhered to so blindly that they cannot but perish in the face of change or it has been tossed aside as irrelevant to the needs of the twentieth century and they are left without so much as an idea of precedence. Increasingly in the post-war world Wharton saw her compatriots as willing to discard their history – both their European and their American past – and attempting to live without a specific geography. It was not simply the war, however, which caused the breach between generations; Wharton had begun to treat the subject much earlier, in her first American novel, *The House of Mirth*, where the luckless Lily Bart is unequivocally 'the victim of the civilisation which had produced her'.[27]

4

Inside the House of Mirth

In 1904, with the successful publication of her first novel, *The Valley of Decision*, behind her, Wharton was about to begin the writing of an indigenous literature, a literature which derived directly from her growing awareness of the unique conditions of social change in the United States. Her Italian historical novel had prepared her for this task, not only in terms of the management of a full-length work of fiction, but also in the aesthetic presentation of cultural uncertainty and its effects on the individual. Just as Odo Valsecca is certain to fail in the new Italy so Lily Bart, the character at the centre of *The House of Mirth*, is, from the very first page, given no chance of survival beyond her power to be, in the original title of the book, 'A Moment's Ornament'.[1]

As Wharton wrote the novel which was to establish her as one of the pre-eminent artists in turn-of-the-century America, the New York from which she came, a community with its boundaries at 32nd and 45th Street and 3rd and 5th Avenue and its suburbs in Newport, Rhode Island and all the major cities of Europe, was about to disappear under the weight of the new money from the manufacturing West. *The House of Mirth* portrays that society's own complicity in its destruction. The novel is, in every way, a 'coming into her own' for Wharton: the social, sexual and cultural apprehensions which were hers find their way directly into the text. As she says in *A Backward Glance*:

> fashionable New York. . . . There it was before me, in all its flatness and futility, asking to be dealt with as the theme most available to my hand, since I had been steeped in it from infancy, and should not have to get it up out of the note-books and encyclopaedias – and yet![2]

Although Wharton always denied that she had 'studied hard' when working on her first novel, *The Valley of Decision* had required immense scholarship, and the lists she made of historical data, archaic phrases and tropes attest to the hard work she put into the planning and construction of the historical *milieu* of the novel. *The House of Mirth*, however, is marked only by a few jottings in her Writer's Notebook and these mainly refer to the naming of the book. In addition to 'A Moment's Ornament' Wharton toyed with the idea of calling her novel 'The Year of the Rose', both titles drawing attention to the central protagonist and the fact of her transience rather than to the society in which she operates and which is the reference for the final title. The discarded 'A Moment's Ornament', which originates in the Wordsworth lyric 'She was a Phantom of Delight', was actually the heading under which Wharton made her brief notes for character and plot and this poem has a number of personal reverberations for Wharton which are enlightening to a discussion of the novel.

In a notebook kept by Edith's mother, Lucretia Jones, when she was in her early teens, 'She was a Phantom of Delight' features as one entry amongst a collection of others on the general subject of womanhood. The poem also features as the paradigm of the female virtues for *Godey's Lady's Book*, a magazine for women with a circulation of 150 000, which just before Wharton's birth was advocating a study of the lyric so that its readers could understand the nature of the '"perfect Woman" which it has been our aim to develop and inspire'.[3] The use of this particular poem as currency was to reinforce the decorative yet domestic purpose of the female; she was to serve as 'a moment's ornament' but otherwise to be contained within 'household motions light and free'.[4] The heroine of *The House of Mirth* is – in theory – an ideal representative of this binary system where the two parts of the female revolve, of course, around the household God. Lily, however, fails to understand sufficiently well that her beauty and her talents are only valid if circumscribed within the institution of marriage and that if 'a girl's as good-looking as that she'd better marry; then no questions are asked'.[5] From the very beginning of the novel we are left in no doubt that the paradigm, the 'perfect Woman, nobly planned', into which Lucretia Jones would no doubt have tried to shape her daughter, has become society's dupe: 'She was so evidently the victim of the civilisation which had produced her, that the links of her bracelet seemed like manacles chaining her to her fate'.[6]

The formula woman of the Wordsworth lyric is not the only culturally prescribed example which Wharton points to in her consideration of the female 'picture' in *The House of Mirth*. Cynthia

Griffin Wolff, in her study of Wharton, *A Feast of Words*,[7] discusses in detail female portraiture in the novel and how it serves the end of presenting women by homogenising the individual into a type. This is achieved by domesticating both the written and the painted word so as to express a sterilised aesthetic which has the woman at its centre, depicted, and therefore controlled, by the male artist. As Peter Van Degan, in the later novel, *The Custom of the Country*, describes it: 'the great thing in a man's portrait is to catch the likeness – we all know that; but with a woman's it's different – a woman's picture has got to be pleasing. Who wants it about if it isn't?'[8] This is the aesthetic of the double standard by which the society portrayed in both novels operates; it falsifies what it purports to represent just as the idea of a coherent and secure dwelling-place – the *House* itself – is denied by the context of *Mirth*.

From James's *Portrait of a Lady* (1881), Grant's *Unleavened Bread* (1900), Dreiser's *Sister Carrie* (1900), through to Phillips's *Susan Lenox* (1917) and Lewis's *Main Street* (1920) – all of which were singled out at various times for Wharton's special praise – the artists of the age were exploring and defining the American scene through its women. Wharton herself is at the heart of this movement and as a woman her vision is actually the most nihilistic amongst those authors named; hers is the only heroine to die and in so doing Lily Bart grimly illustrates Wharton's negative inspiration for the novel: 'a frivolous society can acquire dramatic significance only through what its frivolity destroys. Its tragic implication lies in its power of debasing people and ideals . . . in short, . . . my heroine, Lily Bart'.[9]

In all the novels mentioned here there can be said to be a negative inspiration behind the writing; each author uses the American woman at the centre of the story to show the terrible abyss between the establishment myth of achieved womanhood and the poverty of opportunity presented by a life where the woman is, as Susan Lenox discovers: 'Favorite; pet. Not the equal of man, but an appetizer, a dessert. . . . Not really a full human being; merely a decoration'.[10] As with the society portrait, the positioning of the woman at the heart of the novel is spurious; the reason why she is so portrayed is to reinforce the fact that she is encapsulated in a fixed rôle. In her introduction to the 1936 reprint of *The House of Mirth* Wharton calls the novel a '"conversation piece" of which [Lily Bart] forms the central figure'.[11] This definition highlights the talk of and around Lily who is caught, time and time again, in a series of stereotypical poses in the interpretation of which she has no power to intervene. When we first see her, with Lawrence Selden, at the beginning of the novel, she shows herself to be aware of the terms on which she keeps her place at the dinner table of the rich and, most significantly, of the difference between their respective social worth:

> She surveyed him critically. 'Your coat's a little shabby – but who cares? It doesn't keep people from asking you to dine. If I were shabby no one would have me: a woman is asked out as much for her clothes as for herself. The clothes are the background, the frame, if you like: they don't make success, but they are a part of it. Who wants a dingy woman? We are expected to be pretty and well-dressed till we drop – and if we can't keep it up alone, we have to go into partnership.'[12]

Lily uses the language of visual art so central to the figurative structure of the novel to describe her own position; she knows what the medium of exchange is and that there is no question that the grounds for judgement in this society are entirely material. The formal placing of the woman in the social picture is all-important and should she step outside that frame, as Lily does on a number of occasions, she loses her worth, becoming no longer current or marketable.

Lawrence Selden, Lily's sometime friend and nearly lover, actually makes a limited attempt to take an independent line in his assessment of her: for instance, his first reaction to her representation of Reynolds' *Mrs Lloyd* in the 'tableaux vivants' is original, if self-satisfied:

> It was as though she had stepped, not out of, but into, Reynolds's canvas, banishing the phantom of his dead beauty by the beams of her living grace ... for the first time he seemed to see before him the real Lily Bart, divested of the trivialities of her little world. . . .[13]

Selden is not, unfortunately, alone in his appreciation of the alternative Lily as she sheds her social costume, but the others only take note of the sensual aspect of her living portrait. Selden has – albeit briefly – seen Lily as an artist in her own right; she has assumed the masculine rôle in composing the canvas but he nevertheless appreciates her talents. It is this creative rôle, however, which causes society at large to react against Lily; Jack Stepney's formulation of her being 'up at auction'[14] is not a denial of her being so, it is a complaint against the fact that she looks as though she knows she is. It is left to Ned Van Alstyne – a purveyor of 'after-dinner aphorisms'[15] – to put the social view: '"When a girl's as good-looking as that she'd better marry; then no questions are asked. In our imperfectly organised society there is no provision as yet for the young woman who claims the privileges of marriage without assuming its obligations"'.[16] What he is actually protesting about is the centring of a woman in a picture without the commissioning power of husband or money to put her there.

Selden's subversive view of Lily is not robust enough to withstand group pressure, however, as he almost immediately succumbs to the general opinion when she is seen to be caught in a picture which apparently denotes adulterous guilt. As he walks home with Ned Van Alstyne, Selden sees Lily in a doorway as one of 'two figures ... silhouetted against the hall-light'.[17] The doorway is a frame in more ways than one for Lily who has been lured under false pretences to the Trenor house by the husband of her best friend who is demanding payment in kind for the financial obligations she has incurred to him. Selden makes no attempt to investigate the circumstances behind the composition of the scene he has witnessed; reverting to the ways of society at large, he accepts the appearance, the manner of presentation, as all there is to know.

When Henry James gave his reaction to *The House of Mirth* in a letter to Wharton he said that he felt Lawrence Selden was 'too *absent*'[18] from the text. However, in his own book, *The American Scene*, published in 1907 but deriving from his visit to the United States in 1904, he draws attention to the very 'failure of the sexes to keep step socially' which Wharton is communicating through her characterisation in the novel. He goes on:

> it illustrates further the foredoomed *grope* of wealth, in the conquest of the amenities – the strange necessity under which the social interest labours of finding out for itself, as a preliminary, what civilization really is. If the men are not to be taken as contributing to it, but only the women, what new case is *that*, under the sun, and under what strange aggravations of difficulty

therefore is the problem not presented? . . . This truth points
again the effect of a picture poor in the male presence. . . .[19]

The House of Mirth, deriving from the same time and place as
James's survey of the culture, is 'poor in the male presence', and it
is deliberately so: Selden, as Wharton herself wrote in a letter to
Sara Norton, is 'a negative hero'.[20] As with the title of the novel,
the noun here is contradicted by the qualification, and it actually
fleshes out James's formulation of the deficiencies of the American
social scene if we understand that Selden's absence from the text is
a deliberate part of Wharton's authorial strategy.

The negative cogency of *The House of Mirth* does not derive
simply from the insufficiency of its males, however, but also from
the identification of the dislocation between appearance and reality
in every corner of the social structure. This can be neatly illustrated
by looking briefly at Wharton's reporting of the contemporary
response to the novel, a response which actually mirrors the
hypocrisies which are the subject of the story. In her 1936 introduction to a new edition of the book, she shows us how to read her
text:

> here was a tale written by one of themselves, a tale deliberately
> slandering and defiling their most sacred institutions and some
> of the most deeply revered members of the clan! And what
> picture did the writer offer to their horrified eyes? That of a
> young girl of their world who rouged, smoked, ran into debt,
> borrowed money, gambled, and – crowning horror! – went home
> with a bachelor friend to take tea in his flat! And I was not only
> asking the outer world to believe that such creatures were
> tolerated in New York society, but actually presenting this
> unhappy specimen as my heroine![21]

The public outcry, real enough at the time, although deliberately
rendered ridiculous by Wharton's retrospective on it, is actually
identical with the bogus morality of the society portrayed in the
novel. The obfuscation and the stereotyping which deny any real
rôle to the woman translate her from human to commodity. Such a
transformation is then acknowledged only in the placing of the
woman at the centre of a work of art – Wharton's novel or the
society portrait – which can be openly bought and sold, unlike the

individual woman, who may only be bartered for covertly. It is from this moral base that the woman who acts in spite of the framing of her position must operate and it is such as Bertha Dorset – a brilliant and cruel subverter of the system – who wield their social power as ruthlessly as any successful businessman wields his economic power:

> She was smaller and thinner than Lily Bart, with a restless pliability of pose, as if she could have been crumpled up and run through a ring, like the sinuous draperies she affected. Her small pale face seemed the mere setting of a pair of dark exaggerated eyes, of which the visionary gaze contrasted curiously with her self-assertive tone and gestures; so that, as one of her friends observed, she was like a disembodied spirit who took up a great deal of room.[22]

Within this description, which introduces Bertha Dorset into the novel, Wharton contains the tension between 'pose' and 'setting' and the reality of individual conduct. Bertha is aware, through her putting on of 'sinuous draperies', of her decorative value; her face is the frame which sets off the dramatic nature of her eyes, the expression of which – 'visionary' – is so obviously at odds with the generally sordid nature of her actions. All her attributes are contained by the 'affected': her clothes, her expression and her restlessness or 'pliability', so that, in the spirit of the age, she looks the part in being constructed according to the aesthetic of the female as mere decoration. Bertha herself, however, has gone beyond the limits set by the composition and has become 'disembodied' by stepping outside the moral rôle which is supposed to be contained within the picture. Secure in the large purse and the slow wit of her husband, George, she does just as she pleases with regard to taking lovers, spending money and setting fashionable standards for society in terms of who is admitted into its inner sanctum. It is this woman who ensures that Lily Bart is rejected by the people amongst whom she has always lived. Bertha Dorset's influence is a terrible and significant power because the social life is the whole of life for women in this world, debarred as they are from the professions or even, unless they are self-confessed freaks like Gerty Farish, a real commitment to good works. It is a direct consequence of the inverted structure of the moral system in *The*

House of Mirth that Bertha, being inside the construct of the social picture, can expel Lily from their world for the misdeeds that she, Bertha, has committed; she has 'negative duties'[23] to perform.

The climactic sense in which *The House of Mirth* is negatively framed is, however, in a total inversion of moral values which is only partly revealed by Bertha Dorset. The homogenising intentions of society portraiture are the most obvious example of the fashion to deceive but on close examination the whole cultural picture which Wharton draws is a negative version of an ordered civilisation. Just beneath the smooth social surface lurk modes of conduct which pervert the truth and received principles of behaviour whilst seeming to adhere to them. Henry James, again in *The American Scene*, observed of the social process: 'What was taking place was a perpetual repudiation of the past, so far as there had been a past to repudiate, so far as the past was a positive rather than a negative quality'.[24] James, however, was writing after an absence of twenty years had played havoc with his topographical memories; Wharton wrote *The House of Mirth* with the same sense of cultural dislocation but also with a sense which was enhanced by a strong feeling of personal social supersession. When she talks of those who exert a 'force of negation which eliminated everything beyond their own range of perception',[25] she is speaking from her own whole-cultural disappointment as well as from her rôle as the chronicler of the destruction of Lily Bart.

Lily herself is a survival not a survivor; her mother had 'died of a deep disgust'[26] at the failure of Lily's 'neutral-tinted'[27] father to keep financial responsibilities away from her, and Lily, who had been brought up 'to think of her beauty as a power for good, as giving her the opportunity to attain a position where she should make her influence felt in the vague diffusion of refinement and good taste',[28] is thus bereft of a context in which to operate. She is altogether too feeble to survive in the new world of the twentieth century; her scruples – the feelings of delicacy which prevent her from using to her own advantage the Selden-Dorset letters – are out of place. Ironically, in her efforts to preserve some integrity, she removes to an even more valueless and anarchic setting when she goes as companion to Mrs Norma Hatch, who, in spite of the decadent, nether-world atmosphere of the Hotel Emporium, retains that 'ineradicable innocence which, in ladies of her nationality, so curiously coexists with startling extremes of experience'.[29]

The life Lily finds herself a part of as one of Mrs Hatch's entourage is a literal representation of the underside of society, a nightmarish copy of the world she has left:

> Lily had an odd sense of being behind the social tapestry, on the side where the threads were knotted and the loose ends hung. For a moment she found a certain amusement in the show, and in her own share of it; the situation had an ease and unconventionality distinctly refreshing after her experience of the irony of conventions. But these flashes of amusement were but brief reactions from the long disgust of her days. Compared with the vast, gilded void of Mrs Hatch's existence, the life of Lily's former friends seemed packed with ordered activities. Even the most irresponsible pretty woman of her acquaintance had her inherited obligations, her conventional benevolences, her share in the working of the great civic machine; and all hung together in the solidarity of these traditional functions. The performance of specific duties would have simplified Miss Bart's position; but the vague attendance on Mrs. Hatch was not without its perplexities.[30]

Lily's apprehension of 'the irony of conventions' is not an awareness shared by her employer; Mrs Hatch has no consciousness of acting against a set of principles because she has no principles other than those of pleasure. The metaphor of the inverted tapestry is the crowning example of the negative troping which informs the novel: all the threads which constitute the social fabric are there but the pattern they make is reversed and the rough joins and unfinished ends are all revealed. The picture might look the same from a distance, but once examined closely it becomes obvious that the scene is one of disorder. The lifestyle created by Mrs Hatch signals the next stage on or down for both Lily and society in general as the links between past and present are cut; 'inherited obligations' do not exist, even those which relate to the timing of meals: 'Mrs. Hatch and her friends seemed to float together outside the bounds of time and space. No definite hours were kept; no fixed obligations existed; night and day flowed into one another in a blur of confused and retarded engagements so that one had the impression of lunching at the tea-hour, while dinner was often merged in the noisy, after-theatre supper which prolonged Mrs. Hatch's vigil till daylight'.[31] And it is just because life at the Hotel

Emporium is only a more blatant version of the society which Lily has left behind, and indeed has no pretensions at all towards a structured and rooted code of conduct, that Wharton has to look elsewhere for an example to hold out to Lily as an alternative, 'a vision of the solidarity of life',[32] to take – tragically – to her death.

At a point early in the novel, when she is still secure in the 'little illuminated circle in which life reached its finest efflorescence', Lily is taken by her friend, Gerty Farish, to visit a Girls' Club. Those who live outside her 'circle' have been entirely unknown to her; with only an 'abstract conception of poverty . . . Lily had never conceived of these victims of fate otherwise than in the mass' and her encounter with them provokes an expansion of awareness: 'this discovery gave Lily one of those sudden shocks of pity that sometimes decentralize a life'. The circling and framing of the social world around Lily has allowed no room for acknowledgement of people or place outside its sphere of operation. The girls *en masse* in their likeness to Lily herself: 'innumerable centres of sensation, with her own eager reachings for pleasure, her own fierce revulsions from pain . . .'[33] thus move her – in her surprise – temporarily towards emotional and financial charity. Lily can, at first, only sympathise with their plight in isolation and in relation to her own instincts and needs, but when she re-encounters Nettie Struther, just before her death, she comes to an understanding of the wider social context in which both she and the girls must live.

Nettie has resolved her own desperate situation by a return to the people and values of her past rather than to a rootless and random future. The factor which has made it possible for her to re-establish herself in 'the continuity of life', is the difficult but crucial security of her and her husband's shared knowledge of the past – '"I knew he knew about me"' – his awareness of her life as a prostitute was the enabling principle of their life together. There is no-one with whom Lily can achieve such mutuality; she is a victim of the negative energies of the age as the power-base shifts finally from the collective to the individual. The moral confusion which rages around Lily is, at the last, triumphant in its complete exclusion of her and her scruples, but as a result of her visit to Nettie Struther's kitchen she is granted a vision of a departed world, gone before she could recognise it:

But there was something more miserable still – it was the clutch of solitude at her heart, the sense of being swept like a stray uprooted growth down the heedless current of the years. That was the feeling which possessed her now – the feeling of being rootless and ephemeral, mere spindrift of the whirling surface of existence, without anything to which the poor little tentacles of self could cling before the awful flood submerged them. And as she looked back she saw that there had never been a time when she had had any real relation to life. Her parents too had been rootless, blown hither and thither on every wind of fashion, without any personal existence to shelter them from its shifting gusts. She herself had grown up without any one spot of earth being dearer to her than another: there was no centre of early pieties, of grave endearing traditions, to which her heart could revert and from which it could draw strength for itself and tenderness for others. In whatever form a slowly-accumulated past lives in the blood – whether in the concrete image of the old house stored with visual memories, or in the conception of the house not built with hands, but made up of inherited passions and loyalties – it has the same power of broadening and deepening the individual existence, of attaching it by mysterious links of kinship to all the mighty sum of human striving.

Such a vision of the solidarity of life had never before come to Lily. She had had a premonition of it in the blind motions of her mating-instinct; but they had been checked by the disintegrating influences of the life about her. All the men and women she knew were like atoms whirling away from each other in some wild centrifugal dance: her first glimpse of the continuity of life had come to her that evening in Nettie Struther's kitchen.[34]

I have included this lengthy passage because, contained within it, is the clearest expression of Wharton's most deeply felt personal creed to be found in the fiction. From beginning to end Wharton's writing is concerned with relatedness – with human relations, transatlantic relations, relations between past and present, present and future, relations between human and landscape and between art and society. Lily Bart is dying of isolation; she is defeated by the absence of a 'centre of early pieties', a constant to which she could refer, comparing and measuring experience through her relation to it – whether a literal house or a familial structure – and, most crucially, taking refuge in it in times of crisis. Wharton gives voice here to her feelings about the absence of a female rôle in America and the sexual isolation which results from it. The 'solidarity' and 'continuity' which she is driven, in the emblematic manner of the soap-opera, to locate in the poorest home, are features of a society which has cross-sexual foundations, real relations between men and women such as those which she later locates in the French social structure.

Wharton's art came to be, for her, the clearest statement of self, the constant in a life which hovered between dwelling-places, between continents, between cultures, and a life in which she never ceased to feel the incompatibility of herself and her own partner, Edward Wharton, and 'the poverty, the miserable poverty, of any love that lies outside of marriage, of any love that is not a living together, a sharing of all'.[35] There is an idealised mutuality which lies at the heart of all Wharton's writing; the inevitable disappointment which her characters face in their personal relationships is a microcosm of a larger whole-cultural malaise. The artificial separation of men and women by the American social structure and the nature of the loss which is consequent upon it is epitomised by the sheer, unnecessary waste of Lily Bart and the belated awakening of Lawrence Selden to her true worth. Wharton's next novel of the American scene, *The Fruit of the Tree*, published in 1907, continues this theme in its portrait of Justine Brent, who lives to tell her tale, but whose dream of real, profound relationship founders on the same cultural reef.

The moral obscurity which clouds Lily Bart's landscape is also a feature of *The Fruit of the Tree*, although the much wider social picture of change and alienation which she portrays in the later novel has a diffusing effect upon the narratorial control of the material making it a less cogent statement of theme. Wharton is not content to write the story of 'Justine Brent' – the original title of the novel – as she had written the story of Lily Bart, but embroils her in a number of contentious issues such as euthanasia, the oppression of factory workers by absentee owners and safety at work. The multiplicity of concerns in the novel is actually mimetic in that there is a confusion of aim and direction among the characters which is reflected in the writing, but there is an awkwardness of composition which is not typical of Wharton's best work. This is partly, however, a result of her attempt to give a picture of a factory and its operatives and her real lack of knowledge of such people means that her expression is, in places, patronising. Like Nettie Struther in *The House of Mirth*, the factory-workers are pressed into service by Wharton as representatives of an ulterior way of life.

The novel is set substantially in Hanaford where the young widow, Bessy Westmore, owns the mills which employ the majority of the local population, having inherited them outright from her husband at his early death. John Amherst, the male lead in the novel, comes to Hanaford as Deputy Manager at the mills and in his zeal to improve the working conditions of the factory hands gains access to Mrs Westmore who, to the surprise of all, falls under his influence and marries him. The marriage, however, is assured of failure; once her initial infatuation fades and the child they have dies Bessy resumes her almost total interest in the pursuit of pleasure whilst Amherst works devotedly on the management of the mills and for the betterment of conditions for the employees.

The most important character, both in terms of Wharton's development as a novelist and within the structure of the novel, is a stranger to Hanaford, Justine Brent. We meet her at the beginning of the story when she has been called in to nurse one of the operatives who has been badly mutilated by catching his arm in machinery. It is immediately made clear to us that having been well born and well educated – in a Paris convent with Bessy Westmore – and her family having lost their money, Justine has converted her humanitarian instincts from philanthropy to the more practical pursuit of nursing. She is Wharton's first and only modern professional woman and, most importantly, she is the survivor that Lily Bart is not. In language that deliberately refers us back to *The House of Mirth* and Lily's fleeting reaction to the plight of Gerty Farish's girls, Wharton talks of Justine's work as satisfying 'the need of some strong decentralizing influence, some purifying influx of emotion and activity';[36] she has the rare gift, in Wharton's fiction, of self-knowledge and the capacity to act in recognition of her own strengths and weaknesses.

The lives of these three characters become entwined so that Justine is half employee, half guest in Bessy's Long Island home and acts as moderator between her and Amherst when relations between them become so bad that he goes away and takes a job in a mill in the deep south. When Bessy suffers a near-fatal riding accident that is certain to leave her a complete cripple if she survives, Justine answers her friend's pleadings for death and her own horror at the methods being used to keep her alive with an overdose of morphine. Eighteen months later, when Justine, now working as companion to Bessy's daughter from her first marriage, attends the opening of the Westmore Memorial Hospital, she and Amherst meet again and realise the extent of their affinity. They marry and have a period of perfect happiness united in every aspect of life – their work at the mills and their domestic existence. However, the doctor who was attending Bessy after her accident and who guessed that her death had been hastened, blackmails Justine and when she refuses to help him to a position within the gift of Bessy's father, she feels that she must reveal all to her husband. Justine then removes herself from Amherst and the work at the mills but after a separation of a year they are reunited. It is, however, a reunion on a lower level; no longer does the complete trust of their early married life prevail: 'Nothing was left of that secret inner union which had so enriched and beautified their outward lives'. Justine is forced to adjust her expectations downwards as the consequences of her act of mercy teach her that 'life is not a matter of abstract principles, but a succession of pitiful compromises with fate, of concessions to old traditions, old beliefs, old charities and frailties'.[37]

The disillusion of Justine is complete and is expertly depicted in *The Fruit of the Tree*, but Wharton approached the drawing of the conditions in the mills more cautiously, as the notes in the back pages of her 1905 diary – mainly taking the form of lists of machinery and technical vocabulary – testify. Despite her visits to a New England mill she still made a number of factual errors in the book which were immediately picked up by her readers and corrected in subsequent printings. These mechanical mistakes are merely symptomatic, however, of the overall indecisions in the text which derive from Wharton's efforts to achieve a larger relevance, through a wider social and demographic picture, for her continuing struggle to portray the divisiveness of the American social system.

In spite of the faltering of some of the writing Wharton's concern about the spurious separation of the sexes in her native land still rings loud and clear throughout the text. The position of women like Bessy Westmore, rich and privileged though she is, is shown to be analogous to the factory workers in terms of real economic dependence: neither group participates in the decision-making process. It is an analogy which rests easily with the arguments put forward by feminist writers of the turn of the century, such as Charlotte Perkins Gilman, who talks in her 1898 essay, the 'Economic Basis of the Woman Question', of the fact that 'in our social world to-day, men and women who are familiar with liquefied air and Roentgen rays, who have accepted electric transit and look forward with complacence to airships, people who are as liberal and progressive in mechanical lines as need be hoped, remain sodden and buried in their prehistoric sentiment as to the domestic relation'.[38] In Wharton's novel the cycle of deprivation which forces its victims into complicity by their participation in the process which perpetuates their ignorance is a feature of life both in the home and the mills; for example, Bessy

> had once more dismissed the whole problem to the vague and tiresome sphere of 'business,' ... Her first husband – poor unappreciated Westmore! – had always spared her the boredom of 'business,' and Halford Gaines and Mr Tredegar were ready to show her the same consideration; it was part of the modern code of chivalry that lovely woman should not be bothered about ways and means.[39]

Wharton uses the same fund of language as Gilman who talks of the 'immense anachronism' created by the confinement of women to a single sphere of influence. The 'modern code of chivalry', as Wharton has it, vaunted as an immense privileging of 'lovely woman' is a retrogressive tactic aptly expressed here and else-where in the novel by the vocabulary of feudalism.

The degeneration, the trivialising of women, is made to walk hand-in-hand with the burgeoning of economic and scientific opportunity for the man in the work of both authors; develop-ments which should be open to the whole of humanity are, in a male-dominated language, kept from the woman by the name of 'business' which signifies 'boredom' for Bessy but interest for her husband, father and legal advisor. Wharton's concern is to expose the reasons behind the tactic of exclusiveness and it is worth repeating Charles Bowen's formulation of the custom of the country here: 'In America the real *crime passionnel* is a "big-steal" – there's more excitement in wrecking railways than homes'. Amherst complains that his first wife is unable to conquer the old divisiveness of the American way: 'the ancient ineradicable belief in the separable body and soul! Even an industrial organization was supposed to be subject to the old theological distinction, and Bessy was ready to co-operate with her husband in the emancipa-tion of Westmore's spiritual part if only its body remained under the law',[40] because he has not connected the fact that her inability to see the working life and the social life of the operatives as inextricably linked derives from the fact that she has been brought up with one half of her own capacity completely undeveloped. As Mrs Ansell says, Bessy is 'one of the most harrowing victims of the plan of bringing up our girls in the double bondage of expediency and unreality, corrupting their bodies with luxury and their brains with sentiment, and leaving them to reconcile the two as best they can, or lose their souls in the attempt'.[41]

The figurative language of the novel derives not only from feudalism but also from two further – and contiguous – sources which Wharton melds together to great ironic effect: the first employs the terms of reference of the American Constitution and the second the vocabulary of slavery and the abolitionists. In a previous chapter I discussed the fact that the constitutional separation of church and state in America means, for Wharton, that the domestic and the professional are also subject to the same apparently inalienable divide. Wharton makes use, in *The Fruit of the Tree*, of a number of pairs, yoked by opposition, which stem from this greatest of divides, such as the separation of body and soul cited above or the gap between theory and practice on matters as far-ranging as euthanasia and the status of women. The novel is full of doublings back: of concessions and retractions, of progress and reversion; Wharton moves her characters – notably Justine – so far towards the positive assertion of a personal morality, but when a largeness of understanding fails to come from her chosen partner she has to be content with the secondary rôle which society at large is willing to concede to her.

At the close, the largest separation of all is in the gap between Amherst's sense of what is proper to the spheres of female and male action; much as he may have striven to engage Bessy's attention in a traditionally male area – his work at the mills – his course of action when confronted with a woman who has freed herself from the constraints of the usual is to regress. He endows his life with Bessy with an entirely spurious mutuality, casting a retrospective sympathy of motive and method over the past; forgetting the 'hard small nature'[42] which constrained and made sordid his every move toward humanitarian reform at the factory, he chooses to believe that her plans for the building of a luxurious gymnasium were laid with the workers of Westmore in mind. He has reacted to his own failure to recognise Justine's exceptional qualities with a rewriting of history which will save his pride.

The Fruit of the Tree started out as Wharton's attempt to answer the criticisms which The House of Mirth attracted from the reading – and mis-reading – public. Wharton's biographer, R. W. B. Lewis, tells us that Charles Scribner, her publisher, particularly asked her to take notice of her readership in the composition of character in future writings: 'in your next book you must give us a strong man, for I am getting tired of the comments on Selden'.[43] In an effort, therefore, to compensate for the pejorative response of some of her audience to the 'negative hero' with whom she illustrated the conditions of sexual isolation for the female, Wharton tried to make Amherst a positive and rational moral agent within the narrative. In conflict first with the senior management at the mill and then with Bessy and her family, Amherst is principled and determined in everything he does. When confronted by a woman whose moral strength so surpasses his in its largeness and coherence of thought and action that she appears to move outside even the limits which he has exceptionally granted to her, like Selden before him he fails to make the leap of understanding which would ultimately fortify their relationship:

> His second marriage, leading him to the blissful discovery that women can think as well as feel, that there are beings of the ornamental sex in whom brain and heart have so enlarged each other that their emotions are as clear as thought, their thoughts as warm as emotions – this discovery had had the effect of making him discard his former summary conception of woman as a bundle of inconsequent impulses, and admit her at a stroke to full mental equality with her lord. The result of this manumission was, that in judging Justine he could no longer allow for what was purely feminine in her conduct. It was incomprehensible to him that she, to whom truth had seemed the essential element of life, should have been able to draw breath, and find happiness, in an atmosphere of falsehood and dissimulation.[44]

The admission of Justine into the rank of 'mental equality' is, as Wharton makes plain, a raising of her from slave to human as her 'lord' grants her 'manumission'. However, once having emancipated Justine from the bondage of the category of the 'purely feminine' her fall from grace becomes a personal humiliation for him; no longer can he judge her by the criterion of female ignorance and so he seeks refuge in regression to a romantically adjusted picture of his life with Bessy. The novel begins with Amherst advocating to Justine the mercy killing of the operative whose arm has been rendered useless after having been caught in machinery, but it is Justine's confession that it was the discovery of his own ruminations on the subject of free will which gave her the courage to act on Bessy's pleadings for death that conclusively alienates him from her. To have a woman confront him with the actual physical consequences of his moral speculation is too much for him; the female initiative is what he finds most disturbing as Justine has arrogated the masculine prerogative of endowing or withholding life.

In an unpublished essay fragment, the projected title of which was 'Fiction and Criticism', Wharton writes: 'The novelist ceases to be an artist the moment he bends his characters to the exigencies of a thesis; but he would equally cease to be one should he draw the acts he describes without regard to their moral significance'.[45] *The Fruit of the Tree*, although not planned around a 'thesis', suffers as if it had been; Wharton makes too ambitious an attempt to achieve a comprehensive vision, connecting the demands of an abstract morality with the story too firmly and with a spurious coherence. Justine is given the burden of plot to carry as well as the 'complex vision' of the morally enfranchised. It is this compression of intention which, paradoxically, diffuses the narratorial thrust; Wharton was acutely aware of the opinions of her audience, although she grew to be less affected by them, and *The Fruit of the Tree* suffers because she was afraid to leave anything out.

Elsewhere in 'Fiction and Criticism' Wharton discusses the rôle of the 'moral emotion' in fiction and the attendant need for that emotion to 'confer an aesthetic pleasure on the reader'. The moral and the aesthetic in *The Fruit of the Tree* unfortunately fail to make a connection of this nature but the novel is nevertheless an invaluable staging post on the way to her next American works, *Ethan Frome* and *Summer*. In these novels, both written in France but dealing exclusively with the landscape of her chosen home in the United States, the Massachusetts Berkshire Hills, she achieved a balance between the two concerns, moral and aesthetic, not by complicating and thus obscuring the issues, but by reducing them to their barest level. Wharton concentrates her attention on the limited communities of Starkfield and North Dormer and in so doing achieves a parallel intensity of authorial style and intention.

Ethan Frome and *Summer* are Wharton's most straightforwardly American works of art, not simply in terms of setting but also in the self-referential nature of the social exposition; the comparative use of other cultures, as for instance, France in *The Custom of the Country*, has no place here; any comparison to be made is with a previous America, just as it was in *The House of Mirth*. Unlike her first American work, however, the New England novels are taken up with the bare conditions of survival; the most basic considerations – food, warmth, shelter – are not to be taken for granted here, but it is only when more complicated needs arise – like that of loving and being loved – that real tragedy ensues.

Ethan Frome is a tale related, in the manner of Emily Brontë's *Wuthering Heights*, by a narrator distanced by time and background from the events which took place. In this mode of telling are combined the objectivity of the outsider with the partial intimacy of one who has been initiated into the conditions of existence for the natives, and particularly those of the climate. The actions of all concerned in the drama are portrayed through an understanding of the limitations which govern existence but the narrator's outside perspective means that a wider sense of the tragedy of human waste and suffering is conveyed. The story is simple enough: Ethan Frome is a farmer struggling on the edge of survival and married to his cousin, Zenobia, who had originally come to the farm in order to nurse his mother when she was dying. Zenobia, or Zeena as she is less exotically known, 'had seemed to Ethan like the very genius of health',[46] in those circumstances but soon after his mother's death and their marriage she becomes an invalid needing help in the house so as to preserve her energy for doctoring herself. This help arrives in the unlikely form of Mattie Silver, a cousin of Zeena's recently made homeless by the death of her feckless father, and she and Ethan fall inarticulately in love. Unable to face life apart when Zeena tries to send Mattie away, and unwilling to exercise the necessary deceit to make an escape together, they resolve to commit joint suicide by directing their sled into a tree. This pact goes horribly wrong, however, and the narrator meets Ethan, a broken and lamed 'ruin of a man'[47] and Mattie, whose 'limp immobility' of body is matched by the 'querulous drone'[48] of her utterances, more than twenty years after the event which took their health but not their lives.

When *Ethan Frome* was translated for publication in France it was entitled 'Hiver', attention thus being explicitly shifted from Ethan to the only triumphant agent of change in the novel, the winter. The moral and geographical isolation of the Frome household is compounded by the snow which seems to enclose and freeze every attempt at growth or development. The narrator first becomes interested in Ethan when he is told that the man's ghastly appearance is partly due to the fact that 'he's been in Starkfield too many winters. Most of the smart ones get away',[49] and his own estimation of Ethan's demeanour is as 'part of the mute melancholy landscape, an incarnation of its frozen woe, with all that was warm and sentient in him fast bound below the surface; . . . he lived in a depth of moral isolation too remote for casual access'.[50] Ethan has tasted of the life outside; he has 'dabbled' in matters scientific, 'though they had not gone far enough to be of much practical use they had fed his fancy and made him aware of huge cloudy meanings behind the daily face of things'.[51] But at his father's death he has to drop his education and return to run the farm, and instead of importing his knowledge of matters outside the diurnal reality of life in Starkfield, he keeps it separate, like his trip to Florida, as a symbol of a warmer, more inspiriting and now unattainable way of life. His attempt to create a study in the farmhouse, a sanctum which imitates that 'of a "minister" who had been kind to him and lent him books when he was at Worcester', paradoxically serves to remove the other side of his life even further from him, for when the room becomes 'uninhabitable'[52] in winter so does his intellectual existence.

The pattern of separation between two sides of existence is a repeat of the divisiveness expressed elsewhere in Wharton's American fiction; both *Ethan Frome* and *Summer* concentrate on the dehumanisation of the rural landscape; not only do 'the smart ones get away' but any activity other than that which ensures basic survival takes place elsewhere. There is no room in the Frome household for the decorative as Wharton illustrates with the incident of the smashed dish and, indeed, the banishment of the impractical Mattie. The emotional poverty of the life Zeena leads is cogently communicated by the effect which is wrought by her discovery of the broken pieces:

Zeena stood beside the ruin of her treasure, stiffening into a stony image of resentment. '*You* got down my pickle-dish – what for?'

A bright flush flew to Mattie's cheeks. 'I wanted to make the supper-table pretty,' she said.

'You wanted to make the supper-table pretty; and you waited till my back was turned, and took the thing I set most store by of anything I've got, and wouldn't never use it, not even when the minister come to dinner, or Aunt Martha Pierce come over from Bettsbridge – 'Zeena paused with a gasp, as if terrified by her own evocation of the sacrilege.

'You're a bad girl, Mattie Silver, and I always known it. It's the way your father begun, and I was warned of it when I took you, and I tried to keep my things where you couldn't get at 'em – and now you've took from me the one I cared for most of all –' She broke off in a short spasm of sobs that passed and left her more than ever like a shape of stone.[53]

Mattie's embellishment of the table with the dish, in being representative of the intimacy established between her and Ethan, is used by Wharton to show her difference from the Fromes, her experience outside the frozen world of Starkfield. She understands things in terms of both use and decoration whereas Zeena separates utilisation and value in a way which is entirely sterile. Wharton shows the dish to be painfully inadequate as a vessel to carry the weight of Zeena's emotional investment and the ambiguity of her utterance: '– and now you've took from me the one I cared for most of all –' in calling irresistibly to mind the fact that it is upon the loss of Ethan she should be concentrating her attention, heightens our sense of her derangement even further.

Wharton, in an article, 'The Writing of Ethan Frome', published in 1932, described the human situation in both her New England novels as the 'tragedy of isolation'[54] and there are many levels of such isolation within the stories. The communities themselves are isolated from the wider world, from developments taking place in that world and from its values and perspectives. As Charity perceives North Dormer: 'a weather-beaten sunburnt village of the hills, abandoned of men, left apart by railway, trolley, telegraph, and all the forces that link life to life in modern communities',[55] so is Starkfield, but it is frozen rather than scorched into immobility. The Frome household is cut off from the community of Starkfield, both literally and in terms of the depth of its suffering, and its inmates are even isolated from each other in the extremity of their need.

The conditions of existence for the inhabitants of the summer landscape of New England are no less severe and dislocated than those of the Fromes but because of the season the environment seems kinder and more humanised except when we are reminded of its implacable hostility by Wharton's descriptions of the Mountain and its inhabitants. Wharton consistently coupled the two novels together when writing of her own work – she jokingly entitled *Summer*, 'Hot Ethan',[56] at the time of composition – and in many ways the later story makes explicit many of the concerns which lie behind the text of *Ethan Frome*. Written as it was in France and in the context of the senseless destruction of the first world war, Wharton describes here the conditions under which mankind binds itself to the landscape with an acuteness born of the most painful realisation of human fragility.

Summer, despite the main plot of the seduction of Charity Royall by Lucius Harney, country girl led astray by city gent, is really about the problem of what constitutes civilisation. The same inadequacy or poverty of human relatedness to the landscape as in *Ethan Frome* is conveyed in this novel through a general picture of the decay into which the local architectural heritage – the library, the old houses outside the town – has fallen. North Dormer is suspended in an uneasy relationship between the mountain and the city; it cannot relate to either and still maintain a distinct sense of itself. The presence of Lucius Harney, the enabling principle in the story of seduction, is due only to the general neglect of the local architecturally important houses, and so the human tragedy of the story occurs as a result of the wider cultural decline.

The defeat of the human population by a landscape capable of the extremes of climate represented by the two New England novels is converted by Wharton into another manifestation of the eradication of the social certainty of the late nineteenth century. As the industrial capacity of the whole nation grows so the rural population declines because it is without, as Charity says, any of the channels of communication that put a community into a wider relation with the outside world. Wharton makes much of the quality of the abandoned dwellings which lie outside North Dormer:

The little old house – its wooden walls sunbleached to a ghostly grey – stood in an orchard above the road. The garden-palings had fallen, but the broken gate dangled between its posts, and the path to the house was marked by rose-bushes run wild and hanging their small pale blossoms above the crowding grasses. Slender pilasters and an intricate fan-light framed the opening where the door had hung; and the door itself lay rotting in the grass, with an old apple-tree fallen across it.

Inside, also, wind and weather had blanched everything to the same wan silvery tint; the house was as dry and pure as the interior of a long-empty shell. But it must have been exceptionally well built, for the little rooms had kept something of their human aspect: the wooden mantels with their neat classic ornaments were in place, and the corners of one ceiling retained a light film of plaster tracery.[57]

All the signs of a civilised and reflective society are here for Wharton, who was the author, after all, of *The Decoration of Houses*. The garden was once fenced, its natural beauty disciplined by human enclosure, and the plants which now grow wild remain in the combination planned by the gardener. The controlled organicism of the comparison between the house and a shell evidences further the attention given to the functional as well as to the decorative. The special features of the house attract tasteful and approbative adjectives, Wharton concentrating on the decorative in order to emphasise the relation of the house to the whole history of human design for living. The dwelling, in retaining its outward coherence whilst being empty of a true 'human aspect', is actually representative, in miniature, of the entire community of North Dormer. Too many people have gone – 'the smart ones' of *Ethan Frome* – for there to be anything but a spirit of disappointment left to rule in the lives of those who remain. Charity is spied upon and envied; where there is so little to go round, any good fortune is bitterly resented. There is conflict in the novel between mankind and the environment but there is also hostility between people as the delicate threads which attach them to the half-humanised landscape of New England are broken one by one by those who give up and head for the city.

Without wishing to labour the point too greatly it is probable that Wharton, writing from a France whose landscape was daily becoming more dehumanised by the effects of the war, emphasised the need for community endurance to such an extent because she had so signally failed to commit herself personally to her native land. Although fond of her Lenox home – deep in *Ethan Frome* and *Summer* country – not least because it was the only house she ever owned which had been designed and built under her hand, she never quite came to terms with the bareness of the landscape. For instance, on her return from France to the house, named The Mount, in the Spring of 1907, she said: 'The place looks well, in its dry, spare, *reluctant* New England way, ... but, oh, how the landscape and the life *lack juice*';[58] the process of her expatriation is visible in her every conjuration of the New England scene in these two novels.

Wharton uses the depopulation of the villages of Massachusetts as the centre-piece of the story in *Summer* by making it the theme of Lawyer Royall's speech at the festival of 'Old Home Week' held in North Dormer. This event, described by Wharton as a 'form of sentimental decentralisation', is framed ironically within the story by the fact that the 'incentive to the celebration had come rather from those who had left North Dormer than from those who had been obliged to stay there, and there was some difficulty in rousing the village to the proper state of enthusiasm'.[59] Mr Royall's speech, however, transforms the event from a surface display – of unity, beauty and piety – assumed for the occasion, to one of more profound significance, taking the idea of commitment to the place of one's origin and actively applying it to those who think to return only if they fail elsewhere:

'Most of you', he said, 'most of you who have returned here today, to make contact with this little place for a brief hour, have come only on a pious pilgrimage, and will go back presently to busy cities and lives full of larger duties. But that is not the only way of coming back to North Dormer. ... My history is without interest, but it has its lesson: not so much for those of you who have already made your lives in other places, as for the young men who are perhaps planning even now to leave these quiet hills and go down into the struggle. Things they cannot foresee may send some of those young men back some day to the little township and the old homestead: they may come back for good. ...' He looked about him, and repeated gravely: 'For *good*. There's the point I want to make. ... North Dormer is a poor little place, almost lost in a mighty landscape: perhaps, by this time, it might have been a bigger place, and more in scale with the landscape, if those who had come back had to come with that feeling in their minds – that they wanted to come back for *good* ... and not for bad ... or just for indifference. ...'[60]

The language here is as susceptible to as many ironies and ambiguities as the celebration as a whole, Wharton playing off the lawyer's use of diminutives and sentimentalisations against the current of criticism which drives the speech on. The central text is the exodus of 'the smart ones' to the city but more than this it is the contingent stripping of value and relevance from the country, the expunging of real emotional, intellectual and physical ties to a native place, Wharton's old familiar 'centre of pieties'. As he says in concluding his oration: 'Believe me, all of you, the best way to help the places we live in is to be glad we live there'.[61] Royall himself is the big man in town for North Dormer, but the unanimous granting of such status is irremediably qualified by the general acknowledgement of his failure in the world outside the community. Royall is describing that which he has failed to live up to himself; only disappointment has brought him back to the country and the 'glad'ness he talks of as a vital part of the spirit of any community is entirely missing from his own attitude to North Dormer. He and Charity resign themselves to the country; variously betrayed by the city and its promise of a higher, wider, more fulfilling existence, they settle down to a life where such resignation to the most basic form of duty is the only remaining satisfaction. The 'tragedy of isolation', to return again to Wharton's description of the source of the greatest suffering in *Ethan Frome* and *Summer*, the 'depth of moral isolation too remote for casual access', is what allies Ethan and Charity with Lily Bart and Justine Brent. The two New England novels, however, in being contained within a severely restricted geography, of experience as well as of landscape, provide an example of a detachment which cannot be sustained beyond the nineteenth-century limitations of North Dormer. After *Summer*, her last resort to the pre-war world, it was no longer possible for Wharton to make so entirely literal the 'tragedy of isolation'; the setting from now on had to be unlocalised if it was to be in the twentieth century.

5
The Writing of American Fiction

The first of Wharton's 1920s novels to have a contemporary setting, *The Glimpses of the Moon*, was serialised in the magazine, the *Pictorial Review*, in 1922, before being issued in book form. The novel had been five or six years in the making, the writing of *The Age of Innocence* intervening between its inception and completion. This prolonged period of composition has nothing to do with the complexity of the text but everything to do with Wharton's personal uncertainty about the story in the context of the demands her publishers were still making upon her for another *House of Mirth*. That Wharton paid attention to their advice, as she had in 1907 with *The Fruit of the Tree*, is evident in the very texture of this novel: the central characters, Susy Branch and Nick Lansing, are Lily Bart and Lawrence Selden made over (with Justine Brent and John Amherst liberally applied) and turned out upon the world to demonstrate to an American audience that happy endings were indeed possible.

The very calculated nature of *The Glimpses of the Moon*, and in particular its neatness of resolution, are, however, what actually make the novel deserving of serious attention. In her autobiography, *A Backward Glance*, Wharton records that in 1906, when attending the première of the stage version of *The House of Mirth* with the writer, W. D. Howells, he explained the immediate adverse audience reaction to the play as symptomatic of the fact that 'what the American public always wants is a tragedy with a happy ending'.[1] *The Glimpses of the Moon* shows Wharton gratifying that desire; the references to the earlier novel are woven into the text to correct them, as it were, for the audience, and yet also to emphasise the differences between the two. The situation of the central protagonists – impecunious but well-born, able to see the worthlessness of the social whirl but unable to live without it – is lifted straight from *The House of Mirth*. The only important change

81

in the pattern of existence for these two parasites on the wealth of their more fortunate or less scrupulous friends concerns, however, the extension of the rôle of dependent from the woman to the man. Burdened with many of the same principles and attitudes as Lawrence Selden and, to a lesser extent, John Amherst, Nick is nevertheless forced to compromise himself in order to live his life of quiet refinement. In the competitive leisure world of the twentieth century – and in spite of the appearance of a latter-day Bertha Dorset in the person of Ursula Gillow – it is no longer enough simply to be a man.

The plot of the novel discovers the affinity of Nick and Susy, marries them against all prudent advice, and launches them into an indefinite honeymoon moving between the empty summer or winter houses of their rich friends with a mutual understanding that if 'either of them got the chance to do better he or she should be immediately released. . . . The law of their country facilitated such exchanges, and society was beginning to view them as indulgently as the law'.[2] Needless to say, the moral 'compromises and concessions'[3] which Susy is forced to make in order to sustain their joint existence – mailing letters for Ellie Vanderlyn, the owner of one of their borrowed homes, so that her husband is deceived as to her whereabouts, generally using the resources of other people to make their own lives easier and more comfortable – these wifely devotions, tributes to his masculine probity, eventually drive Nick away from her. During their period of separation both parties in the exchange of vows marital and commercial find alternative, wealthy spouses: an English lord for Susy, and a mid-Western heiress who hails from Wharton's *Custom of the Country* creation, Apex City, for Nick. Susy, however, finding herself less and less willing to return to the parasitic lifestyle she enjoyed before her marriage, determines to break off her new engagement, realising that she still loves Nick and cannot therefore compromise herself in a loveless marriage. She finds a temporary home by agreeing to look after the five Fulmer children while their parents are away but Nick accidentally catches sight of her during this interval and is also, more or less instantly, re-converted to the idea of their marriage:

> In the first shock of the vision he forgot his surprise at her being in such a place, forgot to wonder whose house she was in, or whose was the sleepy child in her arms. For an instant she stood

out from the blackness behind her, and through the veil of the winter night, a thing apart, an unconditioned vision, the eternal image of the woman and the child; and in that instant everything within him was changed and renewed.[4]

With the world around them daily falling apart and rebuilding itself, with their friends sliding in and out of marriage at an equally rapid rate, Wharton re-unites Susy and Nick in a reaffirmation of marriage and the family which delighted the American public to the extent of sixty thousand dollars for serialisation, publication and a film version with screenplay by F. Scott Fitzgerald. In supplying the demand for a *House of Mirth* with a happy ending, the successful union of Lawrence and Lily at last, Wharton wrote as she never wrote again: against the current of the age. She falsified, in the resolution of the married relationship of Nick and Susy, the true direction of her art; such a resolution had not been possible for Lily Bart in 1905 and neither would it be for Nona Manford in Wharton's 1927 novel, *Twilight Sleep*.

Aside from the self-referential nature of her rectification of the Bart-Selden tragedy, however, Wharton's portrait of the twentieth-century social world in *The Glimpses of the Moon* is bitterly drawn and it is in this drawing that the seriousness of the joke which inheres in the romantic nonsense of the novel is revealed. In order to be comfortable, Susy's and Nick's acquaintances assemble and reassemble in groups which can provide more or less the same pattern of existence in any number of different, world-wide locations. The Lansings themselves are 'as mentally detached, as universally at home, as touts at an International Exhibition',[5] as the world has become a uniform backdrop against which the uniform human drama of money-spending and multi-marriage can take place. The conversion of marriage to big business by women disenfranchised from the commercial world and thus forced to imitate its structures and processes within their own allotted domain is by now fully established. The excesses of Undine Spragg's marital adventures pale beside the code of operation of such as Ellie Vanderlyn as she advises Susy, for safety's sake, to announce her engagement to Strefford before divorcing Nick. As Undine might have thought but never would have dared to utter, the dialogue continues:

'Why, Ellie, what on earth do you mean? Not that you're going to part from poor Nelson?'

Mrs. Vanderlyn met her reproachful gaze with a crystalline glance.

'I don't want to, heaven knows – poor dear Nelson! I assure you I simply *hate* it. He's always such an angel to Clarissa . . . and then we're used to each other. But what in the world am I to do? Algie's so rich, so appallingly rich, that I have to be perpetually on the watch to keep other women away from him – and it's too exhausting . . .'

'Algie?'

Mrs. Vanderlyn's lovely eyebrows rose.

'Algie: Algie Bockheimer. Didn't you know? I think he said you've dined with his parents. Nobody else in the world is as rich as the Bockheimers; and Algie's their only child. Yes, it was with him . . . with him I was so dreadfully happy last spring . . . and now I'm in mortal terror of losing him. And I do assure you there's no other way of keeping them when they're as hideously rich as that!'

Susy rose to her feet. A little shudder ran over her. . . .

'I think you're abominable,' she exclaimed.

The other's perfect little face collapsed. 'A-bo-mi-nable? A-bo-mi-nable? Susy!'

'Yes . . . with Nelson . . . and Clarissa . . . and your past together . . . and all the money you can possibly want . . . and *that* man! Abominable.'

Ellie stood up trembling: she was not used to scenes, and they disarranged her thoughts as much as her complexion.

'You're very cruel, Susy – so cruel and dreadful that I hardly know how to answer you,' she stammered, 'But you simply don't know what you're talking about. *As if anybody ever had all the money they wanted!*' She wiped her dark-rimmed eyes with a cautious handkerchief, glanced at herself in the mirror, and added magnanimously: 'But I shall try to forget what you've said.'[6]

This dialogue, and the social portraiture in the novel generally, anticipates the work of writers like F. Scott Fitzgerald and also Evelyn Waugh, whose 1934 novel, *A Handful of Dust*, bears close relation to *The Glimpses of the Moon*. Susy, like Waugh's Tony Last, is presented as a figure out of tune with the age in which she lives, but she is allowed the straightforward advantage of being aware of her dislocation and thus the satirical thrust of the novel is diffused and finally negated. Wharton appears to be confuting the mores of the new order in effecting the reconciliation of Susy and Nick, but the conclusion is an anachronism. The climax of the joke that is *The Glimpses of the Moon* is actually the historical spuriousness of such a closure. The false tidiness of the ending is the bitterest of punch-lines. Such a resolution, impossible in 1905, is even less credible now that the scene is further debased. Where the Dorset/Selden letters were burnt by Lily as a final offering to the moral values of her past, Susy mails Ellie's deceiving missives in numbered order so as to sustain the more or less mutual hoodwinking that forms the new order of procedure.

The Glimpses of the Moon, as Wharton's first expedition into the post-war scene, is ultimately a bad joke; the soft centre of the novel belies the seriousness of the new social and topographical confusion of her compatriots, and denies her own determination to address her art to that which she saw as the present reality. In an article, 'The Great American Novel', published in the *Yale Review* in 1927, she marks out her fictional territory:

> This perpetual interchange of ideas and influences is resulting, on both sides of the globe, in the creation of a new world, ephemeral, shifting, but infinitely curious to study and interesting to note, and as yet hardly heeded by the novelist. It is useless, at least for the story-teller, to deplore what the new order of things has wiped out, vain to shudder at what it is creating; there it is, whether for better or worse, and the American novelist, whose compatriots have helped above all others, to bring it into being, can best use his opportunity by plunging both hands into the motley welter.[7]

The cultural vocabulary of her native land is now fully applicable to Europe, as the international scene is the 'new world' and a new world which is as much a wilderness as the original because it presents again the conditions of geographical and personal dislocation which characterised American beginnings. Wharton is re-enacting the processes of those first American writers who had to invent their own fictional landscapes in her post-war work as the twentieth-century world irrevocably severs its links with the social certainties of the past. In her next novel, *The Mother's Recompense*, published in 1925, Wharton maps out the territory in the clearest possible way; it is as if she is summing up for herself and her audience the relative situations of her own country and of Europe in the periods before, leading up to and after the war. It is, despite the fact that its specific geography is not limited in the manner of *Ethan Frome* or *Summer*, Wharton's most native work. The novel is in the thematic mainstream of American fiction and, in the best tradition of that art, it moves the genre forward to take in the factors which are affecting and changing its condition.

The central situation of *The Mother's Recompense*, and indeed the surname of the family depicted in the novel, Clephane, had been used before by Wharton in a story probably planned and started around 1901, before *The House of Mirth*, and never completed. This projected tale, entitled 'Disintegration', differs in one crucial aspect from the later novel, however, in that it focuses its attention on the husband and child deserted by Mrs Clephane, whilst the second concentrates almost exclusively on the absconding wife and mother. This change in emphasis enables Wharton to paint a picture of the positive maturation of a woman, painful though such a process is, to the point where she can acknowledge and live by a sense of personal responsibility for her own actions. As Wharton had shown in *The Reef*, such self-possession is painfully won and, moving back into the traditional concerns of the novel of her native land, she once again rewrites the American resource of renunciation, treating it through the experience of the woman in a world redefined by international conflict.

When Kate Clephane decides to leave her husband she can find no way of escape except with another man, a way of escape which forces her to give up her child. It does not take her long to realise, however, that life with Hylton Davis approximates closely to life with her husband: 'The asphyxiation was of a different kind, that was all';[8] and she opts for a solitary existence, even in the knowledge that such a course of action makes her vulnerable to all the uncertainties of the socially unplaceable. She goes without the definition – of whatever kind – which would have been provided by her relationship to a man.

Wharton, in *The Mother's Recompense*, explores the female alternative: that which, in the words of Kate Clephane's sister-in-law, the stolid Enid Drover: '"*Female* – . . . is that word being used again? I never thought it very nice to apply it to women, did you?"',[9] is not admitted as a possibility in the language. This partial language also prevents Kate, the solitary female, from being able to articulate her one lapse from the 'long long toll [she] had to pay to the outraged goddess of Respectability'[10] – her affair with a man much younger than herself, Chris Fenno. Conducted during the war when the usual vigilance of the social world lay suspended, this affair ultimately provides for Kate the most telling evidence of her superannuation – her irrelevance as an independent woman, as a mother and as an American – when she discovers that her daughter is to marry the same man. All the old American dreads rise up to taunt her: her fear of the New World's discovery of her 'past' and of the 'incestuous horror'[11] that lurks between her and her daughter. Perpetrated in Europe, the sins of the mother are not, however, visited upon the American daughter who is allowed to retain her innocence, but are bravely borne back to the Old World by Kate with the recognition, at last, of her own personal responsibility, her own age.

Wharton herself concurred with the judgement of one of the reviewers of *The Mother's Recompense* that it was 'an old-fashioned novel',[12] and it is, in so far as she is portraying the plight of the dispossessed woman, dispossessed of all those objects which are supposed to sustain her in life – reputation, home, husband and child. Wharton does this in such a way, however, as to show again the double standard which operates as between male and female conduct in a particular American context. Kate Clephane has simply attempted to exercise her right to the old American way of escape, absconding from personal responsibility into a wilderness, which is, in this case, social and moral rather than of the physical environment. But as a woman – and a Wharton woman at that – she is not allowed to leave the past behind, she must confront it, come to terms with her part in it and, eventually, live by it. The concerns of the novel, ideas of innocence and experience, new and old worlds, youth and age, individual and collective responsibility – familiar American concerns though they are – are enacted within the sphere of the female; the woman is again at the heart of the cultural exposition, only this time she has usurped the traditional place of the male.

In Europe Kate has been kept afloat by the perpetual hope that Chris Fenno will walk back into her life and sustain the myth of her youth, of her escape, because she is without sight or sound of all those things – people and places – which would have fleshed out the ageing process for her. She is able to deny her own generation, beginning each day as if it were unrelated to the past, until her return to America and her final acknowledgement of the consequences of her own actions. Kate is the only character in the novel, however, to develop an historical intelligence; New York expects her to keep silent about her past:

> It was evident that, as far as the family was concerned, Anne's mother had been born again, seven days earlier, on the gangplank of the liner that had brought her home. On these terms they were all delighted to have her back; and Mrs. Drover declared herself particularly thankful that the voyage had been so smooth.[13]

They have not forgotten the past but they refuse to let it inform their present reality except as a negative force, a denial. The 'incestuous horror' which taunts Kate with her own dream of re-birth – as a mother – is the American nightmare and one from which she wakes alone. Her country has participated in the war but instead of maturing to a sense of international relatedness through the conflict it seems even more determined to deny the mutuality of history and its own origins. With no evidence of the fighting literally present in the landscape, they can, like Kate refusing to admit to her age because she is out of context, pretend not to have participated in the world historical event. The only acknowledged difference which the war has brought about for Anne and her circle is that Chris Fenno has undergone a seachange, becoming Major Fenno, increasing his social worth and negating the fact of his humble origins.

For Kate, however, the war does have a significant effect and contrary to her usual portrayal of the conflict as the destroyer of continuity, Wharton, in this novel, shows it to have some of the powers of a healer. Whilst its terrible and tragic side is not ignored, the war is shown as a finally redemptive force for dispossessed individuals like Kate:

> Then the war came; the war which, in those bland southern places and to those uprooted drifting women, was chiefly a healing and amalgamating influence. It was awful, of course, to admit even to one's self that it could be that; but in the light of her own deliverance, Kate Clephane knew that she and all the others had so viewed it. They had shuddered and wept, toiled

hard, and made their sacrifices; of clothes and bridge, of butter and sweets and carriage-hire – but all the while they were creeping slowly back into the once impregnable stronghold of Social Position, getting to know people who used to cut them, being invited to the Préfecture and the Consulate, and lots of houses of which they used to say with feigned indifference: 'Go to *those* dreary people? Not for the world!' because they knew they had no chance of getting there. Yes: the war had brought them peace, strange and horrible as it was to think it.[14]

The war not only enables Kate and those like her to re-enter the type of society from which previous transgressions barred them but it also enables them to understand and come to terms with the reasons for their exclusion. They can now show themselves willing to make sacrifices for the self-same common good that their subversive actions once threatened to undermine. The 'impregnable strong-hold' no longer has the resources to be able to afford to exclude its own, rebels though they have been, as it must forget internal differences in order to present a united front to the greater enemy.

The most enduring effect of this amnesty only becomes evident after the war is over, when it is transformed into a desperate collective urge to live only in and for the present; this is the new innocence, based on denial and ignorance of what has gone before. Only for Kate does the past give her the 'resolve'[15] she lives by and she thus embraces a new mode of renunciation, the giving up of any claim to innocence. Wharton has modulated the old American resource through such as Anna Leath in *The Reef* who was not allowed the indulgence of retreat, to the point in *The Mother's Recompense* where Kate can only live with herself if she accepts responsibility for her own past actions in her present reality, refusing to marry Fred Landers because it would allow her to pretend to be someone other than herself, to wish the past and all its pain away. It is primarily her sense of history which gives Kate the strength she needs. Renunciation is no longer the refuge of the innocent but the faith which nourishes those who prefer to sustain their hard-won consciousness of self and culture.

The presence of Chris Fenno in the novel, at the outset in Kate's hopes and dreams and at the end in her fears and nightmares, is the constant around which her responses are made:

there was Chris himself, symbolizing what she had flown to in her wild escape; representing, in some horrible duality, at once her sin and its harvest, her flight and her return.[16]

His involvement with her daughter ensures that the consciousness of her 'sin' will be with her always and so, conclusively alienated from Anne, she renounces dependence in favour of self-possession; by living the solitary life she can sustain a topography of self.

In her only book of straightforward literary theory, *The Writing of Fiction*, published in 1925, Wharton has this to say about the structure of the novel as she practises it:

> Even the novel of character and manners can never be without situation, that is, without some sort of climax caused by the contending forces engaged. The conflict, the shock of forces, is latent in every attempt to detach a fragment of human experience and transpose it in terms of art, that is, of completion.[17]

The act of 'completion' here is what distinguishes the work of art, and Kate Clephane has, by her own definition, spoken her 'last word; the very last'.[18] The woman is still at the centre of Wharton's picture but she is not placed there by courtesy of the false aesthetic of *The House of Mirth*. Kate is there because she exercises the 'artistic intelligence' which Lily Bart was condemned for, and she does so in such a way as to show the truth of her own situation, achieving a value which is self-possessed and, more importantly, self-esteemed.

Whilst Wharton emphasises the positive value of the process of maturation for Kate, she does not under-estimate its painfulness, particularly in view of the whole-cultural impediments to the development of female self-reliance. *The Mother's Recompense* marks a contiguous stage in Wharton's work where her own self-consciousness, both as an artist and as a woman, fixes upon the question of such value. Wharton's biographer reports comments she made to her friend and sister-in-law, Minnie Jones, after reading one of the reviews of *The Mother's Recompense*: 'As my work reaches its close, I feel so sure that it is either nothing, or far more than they know. And I wonder , a little desolately, which?'[19] The novels of the 1920s, with their great investment of self, are distinct from the rest of Wharton's work in both style and direction and they have been ignored because of these differences. Estimated at 'nothing' by critical neglect, I believe them to justify Wharton's despondent and tentative evaluation – 'far more than they know' – particularly her 1927 novel, *Twilight Sleep*, which has received little praise from any source. For instance, both Lewis and Wolff, Wharton's best and most sensitive critics, join in the use of terms like 'melodrama' and 'overplotted' to describe story and technique in the novel. From their univocal judgement, however, I would wish to dissent on a grand scale; the text has been misread, and misread from the beginning. Taking Edmund Wilson's view in his 1941 essay, 'Justice to Edith Wharton', as typical – '*Twilight Sleep* is not so bad as her worst, but suffers seriously as a picture of New York during the middle 1920s from the author's long absence abroad. Mrs. Wharton is no longer up on her interior decorating – though there are some characteristic passages of landscape gardening'[20] – it is possible to start with the novel's weaknesses and through a discussion of these reach an understanding of its enduring strengths.

Wharton's geographical and social distance from her subject – American life in the 1920s, particularly as it affects and is effected by women – is invoked by Wilson and critics after him as sufficient explanation of the failure of *Twilight Sleep*. Twenty-five years earlier Wharton had tried to pre-empt such criticism of her first novel, *The Valley of Decision*, by a programme of study and research designed to immerse her in the Italian eighteenth century. A similar programme preceded the writing of *Twilight Sleep* and Wilson is right to point to the slightly stilted, slightly embarrassed tone of some of the writing on the subject of society fads and trends. He is wrong, however, to conclude that the fact of physical distance disqualifies Wharton from penetrating beyond those areas which she had to research to the root of the social malaise she wished to portray.

The linguistic devices by which Wharton sought to achieve a period atmosphere in *The Valley of Decision* – the artificially coherent metaphorical constructs and the carefully authentic dialogue – are repeated in her adoption of an equally affected modern language in the reported speech of the younger generation in *Twilight Sleep*. In setting the mood of the novel, however, the portrayal of the religious and health fads which occupy the time and energy of the central protagonist, Pauline Manford, are dominant. Pamphlets and 'New Thought Books' like 'Just How to Wake The Solar Plexus' and 'Psychic Science Made Plain'[21] are among Wharton's notes and summaries for *Twilight Sleep*, and it is this aspect of the culture of 1920s New York that she draws on to show both the intellectual desperation and the futility of Pauline's life. It is here, however, that she fails. The crazes – philosophies of body, mind and spirit – to which Pauline is attracted are ultimately too unimportant; the satirical focus, as in *The Glimpses of the Moon*, is too superficial to carry the weight of her argument and it is this weakness which has been seized upon to condemn the novel, allowing it to be dismissed as the portrait of a culture misunderstood by a writer alien to its topographical subtleties.

The basic plot of the novel, however, takes little account of the research, light or profound, which went into it; like *The Mother's Recompense*, the story concerns one family, although in this case it is extended by Pauline's two marriages. Pauline comes from the mid-west but marries into New York; her first husband, Arthur Wyant, is of an old East Coast family and her second, Dexter Manford, has a law practice in the city. She has a child from each marriage, Jim from the first and Nona from the second, and we join the story when they are grown up and Jim is having difficulties of his own with his marriage. He and his wife, Lita Cliffe – natural successor, with her precipitate name, to *The Mother's Recompense* vamp, Lilla Gates – have just had a child but motherhood has done nothing to assuage Lita's longing for personal and financial independence. In an effort to keep Lita within the extended family, Dexter Manford takes an interest in her which, when combined with his own middle-aged crisis of sexual uncertainty, soon becomes more romantic than fatherly, and they have an affair. Nona Manford, meanwhile, in love with a married man whose wife refuses to divorce him, tries to hold the various fragmenting parts of her family together, mainly for the sake of Jim, her step-brother and the person closest to her. Pauline is completely unaware of Dexter's involvement with Lita as she is engaged in a constant and engrossing programme of participation in cures, causes, scientific housekeeping and physical and mental improvement.

Although Pauline is unaware of what is going on between Dexter and Lita, Arthur Wyant is not and he breaks into Cedarledge, the family's country house, determined to wreak the revenge he sees his son as too enervated and spineless to take for himself. Nona intervenes and is shot and wounded instead of her father. The explanation of the shooting which is then offered up to the public is that she intercepted a burglar in Lita's room and her father only arrived there after the shot was fired. The novel closes with the imposition of an entirely spurious order on the Dexter/Wyant family as Arthur is sent away for a cure and the couples are reunited as age and interest dictate they should be, Lita and Jim taking a tour of Europe and Pauline and Dexter a trip around the world. Only Nona, 'bewildered little Iphigenia',[22] as Wharton describes her, remains, with her wound, alone in her complete knowledge.

No plot summary, however, can do sufficient justice to the source of most critical discontent with the novel and the undeniable centre of Wharton's interest here, the character of Pauline Manford; she, not the plot, is the reason for being of *Twilight Sleep*. The portrait of Pauline who, along with her daughter and husband, is designated a 'reflector' of action in Wharton's novel plan, has been viewed as her creator's bitterest attack on the triviality of female life and interest in America. Blake Nevius, in his book, *Edith Wharton: A Study of Her Fiction*, sees Pauline as a straightforward illustration of Wharton's comparison of the American woman to the 'Montessori infant',[23] in her book *French Ways and Their Meaning*. Whilst the relationship is plain between Pauline's interests and activities and Wharton's complaints about the disbarment of American woman from full participation in the economic life of their own culture, the identification is neither so simple nor so condemnatory as it might at first seem. Wharton's investment in Pauline Manford has a personal dimension; just as Henry James put forward an alternative, America-dwelling self for Spencer Brydon in his 1908 story, 'The Jolly Corner', so Edith Wharton, in *Twilight Sleep*, posits a self-that-might-have-been in the person of Pauline Manford.

The direct connections between author and character are few but telling. The picture of Pauline's first husband, Arthur Wyant, and his behaviour as a spouse, parallels that of Teddy Wharton in relation to both his management of their estate – 'At Cedarledge he farmed a little, fussed over the accounts, and muddled away her money'[24] – and his adultery. Teddy took the loss of the power to manage the Whartons' country house, The Mount, very badly, although it was his ineptitude that made Edith replace him; and whilst the circumstances of his adultery do not match Arthur Wyant's, the attitude of the Wyant family does imitate closely the behaviour of the Whartons who found it very difficult to admit that anything was amiss with Teddy's conduct and attempted to gloss over the fact that he had embezzled a large sum of Edith's money and used it to set up an alternative establishment in which he kept one or even a number of mistresses. Whilst Pauline re-marries and lives with her new husband, the purveyor of her divorce, in New York, Wharton herself settled alone in France, maintaining a distance both personal and geographical from the scene of her married life.

The writing of self does not end, however, with this parting of the ways. Pauline, like Edith Wharton, is an avid and business-like gardener, and, we are told, 'thought it a duty . . . to spread the love of gardening',[25] opening her grounds to the public and the magazine photographer. Wharton wrote books to promote taste in such matters and was always willing to show her own lovingly designed and nurtured gardens. Pauline's efficiency as a country-house owner knows no bounds; her domestic skills are marshalled and directed toward the creation of a house-beautiful. She is empowered by her wealth: 'It had all cost a terrible lot of money; but she was proud of that too – to her it was part of the beauty, part of the exquisite order and suitability which reigned as much in the simulated wilderness of the rhododendron glen as in the geometrical lines of the Dutch garden'.[26] For the author who prefaced her critical treatise, *The Writing of Fiction*, with Traherne's 'Order the beauty even of Beauty is',[27] the drive for domestic order and discipline was as familiar a concern as that for aesthetic harmony. Wharton's biographer tells that the most frequent reaction of Wharton's guests to her various homes was surprise and pleasure at the perfect organisation and comfort of her domestic arrangements. He reports one visitor who 'thought that the house and garden were as perfect as money, taste and instinct could make them, but that they were cold', but another who could 'not remember any house where the hospitality was greater or more full of charm'. Edith herself responded to a compliment on her attention to the details of domestic life with a telling, if modest, self-description: 'I am rather a housekeeperish person'.[28] Whatever the dwelling under her hand, Wharton never ceased to exercise that 'housekeeperish'ness, the attention she paid to the comfort of her guests making up, in many ways, for the fact that she did not have anyone in truly close relation to her for most of her adult life. Pauline's domestic efforts are inspired by her wish to win Dexter's praise for her abilities as a homemaker – 'Intimacy, to her, meant the tireless discussion of facts. . . . In confidential moments she preferred the homelier themes, and would have enjoyed best of all being tender and gay about the coal cellar, or reticent and brave about the leak in the boiler' – and in many ways serve in lieu of the family life she carefully keeps at a distance with her 'definite and palpable facts'.[29]

Those who see in Wharton's portrait of Pauline only scorn and derision underestimate both her sensitivity as a writer and her capacity for self-analysis and mockery. She has seen the danger to women in the social structure of her country – the artificial constraints put upon the range of interests open to her – precisely because she has escaped from it herself. This escape does not, however, mean that she has ceased to be aware of her own involvement; in registering her personal relation to Pauline's way of life by the focus upon Arthur Wyant/Teddy Wharton and the devoted attention to house and garden she shows compassion for Pauline, pity for the woman with no wider creative outlet for her energies. The identification between Pauline and Wharton herself does not blunt the satirical thrust of the writing but adds to it a further dimension – the strong, directional force of understanding.

Wharton places the manic imitation of the 'business' life which forms Pauline's daily schedule right at the beginning of the novel:

'But look at her list – just for this morning!' the secretary continued, handing over a tall morocco-framed tablet, on which was inscribed, in the colourless secretarial hand: '7.30 Mental uplift. 7.45 Breakfast. 8. Psycho-analysis. 8.15 See cook. 8.30 Silent Meditation. 8.45 Facial massage. 9. Man with Persian miniatures. 9.15 Correspondence. 9.30 Manicure. 9.45 Eurythmic exercises. 10. Hair waved. 10.15 Sit for bust. 10.30 Receive Mother's Day deputation. 11. Dancing lesson. 11.30 Birth Control committee at Mrs. – '

'The manicure is there now, late as usual. That's what martyrizes your mother; everybody's being so unpunctual. This New York life is killing her.'[30]

Her 'New York life' is a desperate parody of the New York living of her husband, the successful divorce lawyer, and the activities which fill it are, without exception, professionally and economically irrelevant. It is only by ensuring that she has no time to pause for real thought that Pauline can sustain the myth of purposeful and productive activity. Nona is excluded from her mother –

unless, of course, she has an appointment – because if she had the power to interrupt the myth of busy-ness would be destroyed. Pauline's schedule has to imitate exactly the real thing in order to sustain her sense of purpose. Dexter Manford has a separate domain where the rules are easily upheld: 'So far he had managed to preserve his professional privacy and his professional authority. What he did "at the office" was clouded over, for his family, by the vague word "business", which meant that a man didn't want to be bothered'.[31] The source of Pauline's privacy in the home is the carefully constructed mystique of the time-table; but as no really substantial portion of time is ever allotted to any one activity the breathtaking speed and irreconcilability with which they succeed each other is their only reason for being. Pauline believes that 'an hour is too long for anything . . . the sense of being surrounded by a sudden void, into which she could reach out on all sides without touching an engagement or an obligation, produced in her a sort of mental dizziness'.[32] The horizon which Pauline most fears is empty of activity; the obsessive nature of her attempts to fill her time only emphasises the terrible concentration of self at the centre-point of the female landscape. Once movement for its own sake ceases then the complete irrelevance – the unrelatedness – of the individual to any important collective cause except that of maintaining the momentum stands revealed. Both Pauline and Dexter have taught Nona 'to revere activity as a virtue in itself'[33] without any sense of an ending; to effect any act of closure would be to deny the validity of perpetual motion.

Wharton repeatedly makes comparisons between Pauline's attitude to her timetable and Dexter Manford's expectation of the professional satisfaction which is his birthright as a man. The first symptom of the crisis of sexual confidence which leads to his affair with Lita is discontent with his work:

> The New York routine had closed in on him, and he sometimes felt that, for intrinsic interest, there was little to choose between Pauline's hurry and his own. They seemed, all of them – lawyers, bankers, brokers, railway-directors and the rest – to be cheating their inner emptiness with activities as futile as those of the women they went home to.[34]

It is a source of wonder to him that he can find some relation with Pauline in the shared meaninglessness of their daily lives; he does not expect, as a professional, to feel any uncertainty. It is uncertainty, after all, that Pauline is continually fending off with her perpetually changing subscriptions to someone else's causes, beliefs and ideas. She has total faith in the comforting and comfortable power of the half-truth, ever-renewing trust in the possibility of complete and effortless *happiness* through the pursuit of the perfect system or creed. Wharton emphasises that the excitement which Pauline feels when she encounters a new idea begins and ends with the language in which it is described: 'whenever she heard a familiar word used as if it had some unsuspected and occult significance it fascinated her like a phial containing a new remedy'.[35] Her chief faith is in the power of words to revivify through re-application; wrenching signification from the past, language becomes a source of 'Rejuvenation!'[36] to Pauline and all those like her who have a semantic gulf to fill.

The audiences of 'bright elderly women' whom Pauline addresses, whether on the subject of 'Birth control' or 'unlimited maternity, free love or the return to the traditions of the American home',[37] are all entirely interchangeable, even to Pauline herself, who starts to make her birth control speech at a Mother's Day meeting and only averts a personal disaster by swift self-contradiction. Wharton's satire here, although focused on Pauline's complete failure to make connections between the various activities and causes she supports, does not preclude acknowledgement of the fact that Pauline has been sidetracked into devoting her energies to the matter of 'propagation',[38] kept firmly to female concerns despite her timetable and all the other apparatus of serious 'busy'ness. To believe in both full-time motherhood and effective birth control is not in itself contradictory; it is the public nature of Pauline's stance on these issues which eventually gives her pause, although she still does not realise that the conflict between the two 'sides'[39] of the case is perhaps generated by those who benefit from being able to divide and rule. Ironically enough, her devotion to the theories rather than the practice of motherhood causes her children to be alienated from her at a time when they most need her help and support. When she rushes to hold Nona in her arms after the shooting, Wharton calls Pauline 'the mother',[40] the definite article conveying a final and bitter sense of how Pauline has been tragically distracted from the only occupation to which she could lay genuine claim.

The simple parabolic nature of a story like Charlotte Perkins

Gilman's 'Making a Change',[41] published in 1911, where the argument that some women find motherhood to be a fulfilling profession whilst others do not is the point of the narrative, is not in Wharton's style. She is, in her characterisation of Pauline, expressing the view that one can be interested and even inspired by matters 'housekeeperish' and still have vast resources of energy and interest with which to explore the world outside. Wharton surrounds the notion of some kind of idealised motherhood with irony, not only in her portrayal of Pauline, but also in the context of Dexter's change of attitude to Lita. A reverence for her in her brief but starring rôle as madonna – 'Then, as she lay in her pillows, a new shadowiness under her golden lashes, one petal of a hand hollowed under the little red head at her side, the vision struck to his heart'[42] – overcomes everything else that Dexter knows about her, the incestuous or near-incestuous relation again allows the elder participant to deny their own generation and experience.

Lita, as an orphan, is both the paradigmatic American and also the paradigmatic literary heroine, but she is not at the centre of this story. In the tradition of the nineteenth-century novel – especially as practised by English women writers – Wharton used the solitary status of Lily Bart both to show her helplessness as a woman without family and yet also to allow her a degree of freedom of movement. She cannot, however, in 1927, produce the same effect from the conditions of isolation for the literal orphan. Feeling no relation to people or to cultural precedents, Lita lives only in the present and for the present sensation. She is completely lacking in any sense of bereavement or loss and so Wharton shifts the centre of interest from her to the symbolic orphan, Nona, and in this conveys a sense of the movement of the culture as a whole. The ancestral line from Lily Bart, through Justine Brent, Mattie Silver, Charity Royall and Ellen Olenska to Susy Branch, is transformed by the introduction of Anne Clephane, followed by Nona Manford and, finally, by Judith Wheater in Wharton's next novel, *The Children*, the real orphans giving way to those who are orphaned by their parents' denial of responsibility. Nona, at the end of the novel, wants only to know if she has somewhere she can live with her new knowledge:

Spiritual escape was what she craved; but by what means, and whither? Perhaps it could best be attained by staying just where she was, by sticking fast to her few square feet of obligations and responsibilities. But even this idea made no special appeal. Her obligations, her responsibilities – what were they? Negative, at best, like everything else in her life. She had thought that renunciation would mean freedom – would mean at least escape. But today it seemed to mean only a closer self-imprisonment.[43]

Nona, like Kate Clephane, renounces the luxury of innocence, but without the consciousness of responsibility, of complicity, which Kate had she cannot derive the smallest satisfaction from such an act. She is – and it is worth repeating – the 'bewildered little Iphigenia', the victim offered up to pay for Pauline's professional optimism, her perpetual hope for 'Rejuvenation!' and her own costly and terrible innocence.

Wharton's next novel, *The Children*, is a less intensely felt piece of work than either *The Mother's Recompense* or *Twilight Sleep* and as such is a winding down of her subject. Indeed, the sequence of novels which I have described as Wharton's American works, beginning with *The House of Mirth*, reaches its conclusion in *The Children*, after which she shifts her attention to autobiography, both straightforward and fictionalised. The actual setting for the story is resort Europe, the Riviera, Venice or the Tyrol, but the topographical spirit is transatlantic; that 'new world' which she delineated in 'The Great American Novel' is the insubstantial world of *The Children*. The concerns which shape Wharton's writing in the novels of 1925, 1927 and 1928 find their most straightforward expression in this last novel of manners. In the first place, she switches attention from the female to the male – a development which was to carry on through her writing of the portrait of the artist in *Hudson River Bracketed* and *The Gods Arrive* – the switch thus enabling her to stand back from her subject and look at the other side of the sexual equation.

Martyn Boyne, the novel's central character, is heir to all the cultural uncertainties of his generation but this inheritance no longer predicts the tragic end of a Lily Bart or an Ethan Frome. Martin has been attached to a woman, Rose Sellers, through the many years of her loveless marriage to another man; as an engineer, his work has taken him to the developing countries of South America whilst she has remained in New York, waiting to become a widow. As the novel opens he is crossing the Atlantic on his way to join her, on holiday in the Dolomites after her recent bereavement. The two words which describe his relationship with

Rose are those which actually define her in relation to another man – 'wife' and 'widow'; she has been faithful to the intention and meaning of the first and expects, not unreasonably, to be rewarded for such fidelity with only a brief sojourn in the domain of the latter. The process by which Martin comes to realise that the sexual and social evasions which 'wife' (when the 'wife' in question belongs to another husband) allowed him are no longer tenable, is paradoxically, through the discovery of a family life, or at least, the company of *The Children*. His involvement with the Wheater children replaces his vaunted commitment to Rose. He has been her husband in waiting, but is distracted from the expected resolution of their relationship by the chance of another temporary engagement. The pattern of his professional existence, a series of assignments or contracts in various and wide-ranging locations, is imitated in his personal life.

On the transatlantic voyage which is taking him to Rose, Martin meets the seven children who loosely belong to the Wheater family. He knows Cliffe Wheater, father of five of the children, from Harvard, and his wife, Joyce, mother of four of the children, from post-college days, and so he befriends the children who are travelling to Europe to join their parents. *The Children* themselves are fifteen-year-old Judith, the eldest, who has 'never been a child – there was no time',[44] next in line are the twins, Terry and Blanca, these three belonging to the first marriage of Cliffe and Joyce; the two 'steps' – Bun and Beechy – follow chronologically if not biologically on, being the children of the Italian nobleman, Prince Buondelmonte, and the wife before Joyce Wheater, Joyce having undertaken to look after them on her re-marriage to Cliffe; next is Zinnie, the result of Cliffe's brief marriage to the film-star, Zinnia Lacrosse; and finally, Chipstone, the baby, who is the product of the Wheaters' reunion. The uncertainty and dismay which is the result of this marital free-for-all for the children touches Martin and he becomes involved in their bid to remain together whilst the Wheaters *et al.* battle it out. They adopt him, he is their chosen parent, and he also uses the fact of their attachment to him to suspend his union with Rose. The plight of the children and his temporary parenthood give him an excuse to postpone consideration of an enduring, adult commitment.

Martin is, in many ways, the archetypal American protagonist. Wharton in Kate Clephane and Pauline Manford showed different female responses to cultural conditioning; here she highlights the

other side, the incapacity of the American male for relationship –
emotional, sexual or parental. At the beginning of the novel Martin
describes himself as 'an old fogey out of the wilderness'[45] but his
terminology is brought up-to-date by the children's governess
when he attempts to repeat this self-formulation: '"The wilderness? The real wilderness is the world *we* live in; packing up our
tents every few weeks for another move. . . . And the marriages
just like tents – folded up and thrown away when you've done
with them"'.[46] The 'wilderness' is thus all around them; it is a
condition of existence and it is the determination of the children to
create some form of stability from such topographical uncertainty
which first engages Martin's interest. For him the children are
re-vivifying the American spirit, seeking to create something
'stronger than the sum of such heredities'.[47] They have parents
and yet no parents – the figure with the most potency as a father
being Martin, the pioneer fresh from his spell in the wild – and
they exercise their rights as Americans to choose him as their
guide. He is momentarily their hero, their model, but when the
inevitable break-up comes, the fragmentation of the fragile barrier
they have erected against the current of the age, Martin can only
retreat from the responsibility of defending the alternative family
they have tried to create.

Martin uses his feelings for the children to dispel the sense of
obligation which binds him to Rose Sellars but his attempt at
parenting is brought to an abrupt end when that once fatherly
concern expresses itself as sexual interest. Judith's interpretation of
his marriage proposal as an offer of adoption shatters any brief
delusions he might have about his ability to commit himself to a
relationship. Thus, at the end of the novel, he is confirmed as the
man to whom nothing will ever happen. The nomadic professional
lifestyle, the avowed attachment to the unattainable lady, the
inevitably temporary nature of his engagement with the problems
of the children, and, finally, the emotional investment in Judith, all
these are the result of his desire to keep real, enduring relationship
out of his life.

Martin comes to realise the fact of his own, willed, isolation only
in offering himself where he knows he will not be accepted; there
is no equivocation on Wharton's part, no sense that the future will
hold anything for Martin but the professional detachment he has
always maintained. She ends the novel with a directness hitherto
avoided in American literature:

> Two days afterward, the ship which had brought him to Europe started on her voyage to Brazil. On her deck stood Boyne, a lonely man.[48]

The three-word closure defines Martin finally; as he lights out for half-known territory, there is no possibility of another ending to his life. The picture is now complete, but it is still 'poor in the male presence'.

From *The House of Mirth* to *The Children* Wharton plots and develops the cultural conditions which rend nineteenth- from twentieth-century America. Despite the fear she expressed in 1918 that the only form of fiction tenable in the post-war world would be the historical novel, she was not ultimately afraid to grapple with the conditions of social transition in her writing. She brought the landscape of American fiction into the twentieth century, an achievement which was recognised and acknowledged by the coming generation of writers. As F. Scott Fitzgerald said: 'Edith Wharton . . . she's a very distinguished *grande dame* who fought the good fight with bronze-age weapons when there were very few people in the line at all';[49] she had to re-invent not only the world in the 'after-war welter',[50] but the means of communication. It was, however, a task for which she had been well-prepared; having always been open to the strenuous demands of work in different genres, one of her greatest resources was her willingness to experiment, this being most obvious in her various attempts to portray the artist, whether in self-portrait or in fiction. Throughout her life she made many attempts at the writing of self, both in straightforward autobiography and fictionalised accounts of her life, and in order to do so she explored a metaphoric landscape – 'The Land of Letters'[51] – as she describes it in her published autobiography, *A Backward Glance*. Those works which are concerned with the development of the artist have as great a determining topographical presence as the more specific geographies of Italy, France and America and provide further insights into the manner and means of her art.

6

'Literature' or the Various Forms of Autobiography

In her autobiography, *A Backward Glance*, published in 1934, Wharton describes in topographical terms the elation she felt at the publication of her first collection of short stories:

> At last I had groped my way through to my vocation, and thereafter never questioned that story-telling was my job, though I doubted whether I should be able to cross the chasm which separated the *nouvelle* from the novel. Meanwhile I felt like some homeless waif who, after trying for years to take out naturalization papers, and being rejected by every country, has finally acquired a nationality. The Land of Letters was henceforth to be my country and I gloried in my new citizenship.[1]

There are a number of texts which together form an enlightening and intriguing sequence, charting Wharton's developing interest in exploring the 'Land of Letters' or the terrain of the artist, and these manifest various degrees of autobiographical involvement.

The first attempt which she made to understand her own early development through her writing was to translate it into a fictional portrait of the imaginative growth of a male child in a novel fragment called 'Literature', written around 1913. Although she plotted the story of the budding artist's life in some detail, only eight chapters were completed before she abandoned the project entirely. Wharton's next autobiographical venture, 'Life and I', probably dating from 1922, was a straightforward account of her own experience which, like the novel fragment 'Literature', comes to an end as the child reaches adulthood. In the two published novels which continue the autobiographical strain – *Hudson River Bracketed* (1929), and *The Gods Arrive* (1932) – her artist, Advance Weston, is on the verge of manhood when we begin the story, this shift in emphasis being sufficient to change significantly the directional flow of her autobiographical involvement. Nevertheless, these novels, and the formal autobiography, *A Backward Glance*, a reticent and distant account of her life, constitute a vital part of the whole picture of Wharton's writing of the artist and the self. She experimented with various forms of retelling her own experience and to compare and contrast these complementary texts is to gain an insight into her own exegesis of the processes of creativity.

Wharton's earliest attempt to explore her own origins and inspiration as a writer comes in the unfinished novel, 'Literature', where she re-enacts, through the hero of the piece, Richard Thaxter, many of her own childhood memories. Those highspots of insight and excitement to which she returns again and again when writing of her own youth are searched for significance and meaning through the story of the little boy, Dicky. Of the seventy-five extant typescript pages of the novel, sixty are concerned with childhood; Wharton's interest in the project falls off as Thaxter grows up. Ten years later in 'Life and I' she again stops short at maturity, her experiences as a child seeming to allow her powers of recollection an uncontentious freedom which does not extend to the portrayal of her adult life. This is nowhere more obvious than in the reserved tones of *A Backward Glance*, the sanitised, official version of her life, where even her explanation for the autobiographical act denies that any previous attempts have been made:

> If anyone had suggested to me, before 1914, to write my reminiscences, I should have answered that my life had been too uneventful to be worth recording. Indeed, I had never even thought of recording it for my own amusement, and the fact that until 1918 I never kept even the briefest of diaries has greatly hampered this tardy reconstruction.[2]

So, contained within her very apologia is the disavowal of any previous autobiographical attempt, to say nothing of her diaries for 1905, 1906, 1908, and the 'Love Diary' – titled 'The Life Apart (L'Ame Close)'[3] – in which she recorded her affair with the American journalist, Morton Fullerton. Although she gainsaid in public her previous attempts at recording her own history Wharton did leave them intact, enabling future generations to contradict the apparently incontrovertible assertions of *A Backward Glance* by simple comparison. The final autobiographical statement can be looked at alongside earlier writings and the process of change in her self-presentation revealed. To borrow Wharton's own image of precedence from 'Life and I', an image of recurring significance both here and in 'Literature' – 'It is difficult, of course, to disentangle these from the palimpsest of later impressions received in the same scenes'[4] – the formal autobiography overlays the previous writing like a 'palimpsest'. The layers of writing the self are separable and can be extrapolated from their position behind *A Backward Glance* to demonstrate the process of Wharton's recording of personal experience. Both the divergences and likenesses of emphasis between versions can be shown explicitly and what would otherwise be obscured and laid over with the language and attitudes of the writer's old age can stand revealed, the final portrait lifted to show the course of its development.

Just as *A Backward Glance* puts the finished, disingenuously polished, seal upon the incomplete and unacknowledged 'Life and I', so the two novels which have the writer, Advance Weston, as their subject, in some measure continue and complete what was begun in 'Literature'. In response to a letter from her friend, Elisina Tyler, which praised the recently published *Hudson River Bracketed*, Wharton made explicit the connection between her earlier attempt to portray the development of the artist in 'Literature' and the later novel:

> It is a theme that I have carried in my mind for years, and that Walter [Berry] was always urging me to use; indeed I had begun it before the war, but in our own milieu, and the setting of my youth. After the war it took me long to re-think it and transpose it into the crude terms of modern America; and I am happy to think I have succeeded.[5]

In telling the story of Richard Thaxter, Wharton wrote out of her own experience, distancing herself from the text by means of a change of sex, but using her own background, her own memories. In the later portraits of the artist, *Hudson River Bracketed* and *The Gods Arrive*, she moved completely away from her own *milieu*, both temporally and geographically, and in so doing exacerbated the conditions of difficulty for the growth of the creative imagination in her subject, Advance Weston. This movement from the turn-of-the-century social certainty of Richard Thaxter's world to the post-war setting of Euphoria, Illinois, and Vance 'born into a world in which everything had been, or was being, renovated',[6] is coincident with the change in Wharton's autobiographical style. From the opening up, the exploration of experience in 'Life and I', to the reticences and occlusions of *A Backward Glance*, the movement is one from recollection and wonder to recollection and conviction, a movement which can be most profitably examined by working back through the formal autobiography to 'Literature' and 'Life and I', and forward again from there to the two Vance Weston novels.

A Backward Glance exudes a sense of complete authorial control over the past; Wharton makes the substance of her memories practically incontestable by describing her position as that of a survivor: 'The compact world of my youth has receded into a past from which it can only be dug up in bits by the assiduous relic-hunter; and its smallest fragments begin to be worth collecting and putting together before the last of those who knew the live structure are swept away with it'.[7] This much-vaunted certainty rests uneasily, however, with one of her central aims in *A Backward Glance*: to emphasise how many difficulties her otherwise privileged background and upbringing threw in the way of her development as an artist. There is a strong tension generated by the conflict between her urge to celebrate unequivocally the social certainties of her childhood world and the desire to convey a sense of the prodigious nature of her literary achievement. The language of the autobiography is consistently embattled: 'I had to fight my way to expression through a thick fog of indifference',[8] such 'indifference' being repeated in the enervated attitude of old New York to all art, except when practised by such as Washington Irving or Longfellow.[9] Not only are her fellow Americans determined to remain ignorant of matters aesthetic, however, their apathy extends also to the political life of the country as a whole, and, crucially, to the changing face of the social and economic world around them. As she demonstrated in novels like *The Custom of the Country*, the failure of her class to participate is the cause of its own extinction.

One of the ironies of Wharton's presentation of her struggle towards artistic expression is that she is forced – because she is concerned always to display her difference – to align herself with the new money, 'the lords of Pittsburgh',[10] whose entry into the New York world of her childhood is shown to be the first catalyst of social change. Despite her attempts to commemorate, even consecrate, the civilisation which has passed away, the intention is constantly undercut by the enduring strength of remembered resentment against the restrictions which were placed upon her, restrictions which actually find a parallel in old New York's initial treatment of the 'Invaders'[11] from the west. Wharton intends that the reader of the autobiography should be drawn into complicity with her judgements. Her vocabulary is qualitative when describing the world of her childhood – 'standards of honour and conduct', 'the value of duration', 'moral wealth'[12] – estimations which proceed directly from her mature autobiographical standpoint, but the nostalgia which sets the tone of her broader reminiscences is not equal to the energy generated by her remembrance of slights past.

Wharton uses a variety of techniques to try to offset the negatives, the deprivations, of her background, chief amongst these being her documentation of the case histories of artists or would-be artists who never had to struggle with an unco-operative or obtuse family in order to develop or practise their creative calling. These examples come in two varieties – the first concerning the literary spouse and the second the literary offspring – and both emphasise Wharton's exceptional and superior achievement. A luncheon with the English novelist, Mrs Meynell, is described in terms which prepare the reader for a resounding affirmation of the circumstances of Wharton's own domestic situation:

> The first time I lunched at Mrs. Meynell's I was struck by the solemnity with which this tall thin sweet-voiced woman, with melancholy eyes and rather catafalque-like garb, was treated by her husband and children. Mr. Meynell, small and brisk, bustled in ahead of her, as though preceding a sovereign; and all through the luncheon Mrs. Meynell's utterances, murmured with soft deliberation, were received in an attentive silence punctuated by: 'My wife was saying the other day,' 'My wife always thinks' – as though each syllable from those lips were final.
>
> I, who had been accustomed at home to dissemble my literary pursuits (as though, to borrow Dr. Johnson's phrase about portrait painting, they were 'indelicate in a female'), was astonished at the prestige surrounding Mrs. Meynell in her own family; and at the Humphrey Wards' I found the same affectionate deference toward the household celebrity.[13]

Wharton renders Mrs Meynell ridiculous by making her an object of sterile, ceremonial worship; Mr Meynell, 'small and brisk', is the devoted high priest, mediating her opinions to the world. The movement and terms of reference of the description ensure that we reject the idea of the pampered and revered literary wife in favour of Wharton's own discrete wielding of the pen. She does not wish to be identified with the affected literariness of the two ostentatiously feminine authors she cites here. The intellectual incompatibility between Wharton and her husband, which ensured that her work remained a solitary pursuit, finds no direct expression in the published autobiography but it nevertheless underlies the vehement nature of her rejection of the special status afforded to Mrs Meynell and Mrs Ward; she is emphasising both her independent achievement and her individual strength.

For a direct expression of the misery which she suffered as a result of Teddy Wharton's inability to engage with her literary interests it is necessary to look elsewhere, for example, in 'The Life Apart' diary where she describes her feelings at his response to her request that he read a passage from Lock's *Heredity and Variation*, 'The answer was: "Does that sort of thing really amuse you?" I heard the key turn in my prison lock. That is the answer to everything worth while! Oh, Gods of derision! And you've given me over twenty years of it!'[14] The agony of isolation which this encounter details has been put aside, if not forgotten, by the writer of the official life; the fact of her own singularity remains but it is turned to good and cheerful effect through the caricature of the literary lady at home. In the description of her work as thriving without encouragement or sanction, Wharton is able to prove, with modesty, that hers is the truly exceptional talent.

Whilst Mrs Meynell and Mrs Ward are easy targets for Wharton in the process of affirming retrospectively the circumstances of her own family situation it is even simpler for her to find foils among her compatriots to set off her own brightness. Such a one is George Cabot (Bay) Lodge, whose position in the autobiography is not only determined by his exemplary rôle as the man designed and nurtured by his family to be an artist and conspicuously failing to become one, but also as the paradigm of a whole generation of American men who, despite their great abilities, fail to achieve anything of note. The book is full of such cases and consistent in its use of a precipitous language to describe them. Lodge, for instance, is in a 'state of brilliant immaturity', 'he would eventually have developed', 'he was simply intended to be', and Wharton leaves us in no doubt that the 'hot-house of intensive culture'[15] in which he was forced causes him to remain permanently on the brink of achievement. There is a blend of sympathy and self-interest in the bias of her presentation; she feels regret for the failure of so many of her contemporaries but is nevertheless willing to use them to highlight the fact of her own success. She is shown to triumph not only in the context of the philistinism of her family but also as a woman; she is given none of the special treatment afforded to the literary wife in her examples and succeeds when all those carefully nurtured and cossetted males around her remained 'in ineffectual ecstasy before the blank page or the empty canvas'.[16]

The direction of Wharton's writing in *A Backward Glance* is relentlessly towards an affirmation of the conditions of her background and upbringing. The old sense of bitterness remains but it has been largely overwhelmed by the struggle to convert deprivation to approbation. When discussing the fact that she was permitted, by her mother, to read any form of literature but the novel, for example, she is able to convert what was an arbitrary taboo to the good: 'Her plan was certainly not premeditated; but had it been, she could not have shown more insight'.[17] Only once does Wharton neglect to close her description of a feature of her education with a positive interpretation; the usual description of the failure of her parents to provide her with sufficient intellectual nourishment is not subject to any but the most half-hearted retrospective justification:

Being deprived of the irreplaceable grounding of Greek and Latin, I never learned to concentrate except on subjects naturally interesting to me, and developed a restless curiosity which prevented my fixing my thoughts for long even on these. Of benefits I see only one. To most of my contemporaries the enforced committing to memory of famous poems must have forever robbed some of the loveliest of their bloom; but this being forbidden me, great poetry – English, French, German and Italian – came to me fresh as the morning, with the dew on it, and has never lost that early glow.

The drawbacks were far greater than this advantage. But for the wisdom of Fräulein Bahlmann, my beloved German teacher, who saw which way my fancy turned, and fed it with all the wealth of German literature, from the Minnesingers to Heine –

but for this, and the leave to range in my father's library, my mind would have starved at the age when the mental muscles are most in need of feeding.[18]

This criticism is exceptional in *A Backward Glance* for its starkness; past feelings are still so powerfully present in the act of writing that they overwhelm the tone. Elsewhere in the text Wharton encircles any such memories of deprivation with pronouncements of maturer wisdom: 'I have thought this over many times', 'as I have grown older my point of view has necessarily changed', and excludes any possibility of further discussion with 'The conclusion is'.[19] Although it seems to be documenting a process of consideration, her writing has no validity as an argument because of the relentless drive towards affirmation. She domesticates her struggle towards artistic expression by making it synonymous with the established fact of herself as the successful writer; even the brief loss of control on the subject of her lack of formal education cannot compare with the real bitterness of such comments as she makes on her upbringing – and specifically her mother's treatment of her – in 'Life and I':

> the only result was that I had been convicted of stupidity for not knowing what I had been expressly forbidden to ask about, or even to think of! . . . I record this brief conversation, because the training of which it was the beautiful and logical conclusion did more than anything else to falsify and misdirect my whole life. . . .[20]

All things are turned to advantage in the redaction of her childhood and education in the formal autobiography, and it is only by looking underneath its all-concealing manner and examining each contributory layer that a broader picture can be revealed. Even the movement away from her background into a world of her own making – 'the Land of Letters' – is not depicted as a liberation or an escape in *A Backward Glance*; the feelings of the aspiring writer in the act of separation are overlaid with Wharton's old-age reverence for the vanished New York of her childhood. The necessary beginnings and foundation of her career have been established as being located in the fact that she is a cultural anomaly, but without invalidating the culture itself.

The commemoration of the culture rests uneasily alongside another act of retrospective justification and that is Wharton's portrayal of her decision to live abroad. The creative paralysis which seized some of her contemporaries, whether as artists or in terms of the wider culture, is pressed into service to explain her removal to Europe, as is her description of the fact that her activities as an author were looked upon as 'a kind of family disgrace, which might be condoned but could not be forgotten'. She is casually ironic: 'it was amusing to think that, whereas in London even my modest achievements would have opened many doors, in my native New York they were felt only as a drawback and an embarrassment'.[21] The mock-humility of the language explains why she, the exception but also the pariah, had to take her 'modest achievements' elsewhere so as to allow New York to live in peace with its prejudices. The mildly sardonic tone allows Wharton to escape blame for her exile whilst also not seriously undermining the larger virtues of a society which 'held literature in great esteem,' but 'stood in nervous dread of those who produced it'.[22]

There are affirmations in *A Backward Glance* which are more straightforwardly enacted than Wharton's belated appreciation of the social structure of her childhood New York and such an affirmation is her portrait of her close friend, Walter Berry. This is not to say, however, that the unequivocal celebration of Berry in the formal autobiography has been easily and painlessly arrived at without prior working-out of the nature of their relationship. Both her earlier autobiography and her fiction bear witness to the fact that there were problems to be resolved before she could celebrate so wholeheartedly Berry's influence in her life but his positive presence is so acutely needed in the text that the developmental process cannot actually be discerned in the writing.

Wharton claims at the beginning of *A Backward Glance* to have nothing malicious to say about anyone in her life story, no enemies to speak of nor injuries which she cares to detail. The absence of the negative impetus to her writing, however, is paralleled by the difficulty she has in finding someone to make exceptional in her life, to put at the centre of emotional significance. Her husband, Teddy Wharton, features only twice in the text – apart from his inclusion in the 'we' of her travels and house-building at Lenox – once at the time of her marriage when she mentions his age, hobbies and liking for Newport, and once more towards the end of the book when explaining the sale of her house, The Mount, as partly a result of the 'creeping darkness of neurasthenia',[23] which was overcoming him. In both instances she immediately goes on to talk about other friends, namely Egerton Winthrop and Mary and Bernard Berenson, and their influence upon her; Teddy is discounted entirely as a source of interest to those who are concerned with her growth and development as an artist or even as a person. In contrast to the space which she allots to Teddy a whole chapter is devoted to Henry James and to a description of the bond of humour and affection which drew them together. Whilst James is celebrated as a friend, however, Wharton takes pains to emphasise that he could not bear to discuss his work with her and was an intolerant reader of her fiction, thus making him ineligible to fill the rôle of the supreme mentor/friend so crucial to her self-portrait. The absence of a wholly satisfactory relationship with a man – even though most of her friends were male – left her with an emotional void at the heart of *A Backward Glance*; she could not affirm the positive influence of her husband or family in either a professional or a personal context and her relationship with the greatest of her contemporaries was also moderated by too many restraints for its presentation to be unequivocal. Morton Fullerton, the American journalist with whom she had an affair – of the mind as well as the heart – could have no place in her published autobiography for reasons of discretion, and so she was forced to come back to her first friend of 'soul', Walter Berry. His influence could be presented, without any difficulties of language, as crucial to both sides of her life; he could be described in terms of complete fulfilment and consummation paradoxically because he was neither husband nor lover, nor even fellow artist.

In the formal autobiography Wharton seeks to define herself in terms of Berry's influence, his constructive influence, upon both her personal and creative life:

> I cannot picture what the life of the spirit would have been to me without him. He found me when my mind and soul were hungry and thirsty, and he fed them till our last hour together. It is such comradeships, made of seeing and dreaming, and thinking and laughing together, that make one feel that for those who have shared them there can be no parting.[24]

Such an affirmation of his active rôle in her development – 'He found me', 'he fed them' – is only possible, however, because she has already worked through the difficulties of their friendship in the fiction, exploring, from a safe distance, the most positive aspect of their relationship, which was that between creative artist and critic. The part which the Berry figure plays – arbiter, critic, aesthete – is vital to the growth of the artist both in the planned scenario for 'Literature' and in the Vance Weston novels, but, again in both cases, there is evident authorial uncertainty as to the possibility of achieving an equity of interest in the relationship.

In Wharton's 'Literature' notebook, which dates from about 1913, are transcribed the first stirrings of one Caspar Levick, 'a genius without creative faculty', whose importance in the novel is projected to be in terms of his influence upon Richard Thaxter:

> The brilliant Levick – Socratic encyclopaedic old man – a rare critic and hack journalist – who wakens Richard's literary consciousness, develops and stimulates him; and then cannot forgive him for being a creative artist and achieving the expression the other has always failed to attain.[25]

Just as in *Hudson River Bracketed* Wharton describes George Frenside, critic and magazine editor:

> the critical faculty outweighed all others in him, and, as he had often told [Halo], criticism won't keep its man. He saw (he also said) the skeletons of things and people: he was a walking radiograph. God knows he didn't want to be – would rather not have had a decomposing mind.[26]

and Walter Berry, in *A Backward Glance*:

> Walter Berry was born with an exceptionally sensitive literary instinct, but also with a critical sense so far outweighing his creative gift that he had early renounced the idea of writing.[27]

The movement of the three descriptions is from resentment to renunciation. Levick's effective encouragement of Richard leads only to his personal realisation that, as a critic, he must always be content with a rôle which is secondary to that of the creator; his achievement will only ever be made manifest by Richard's success. The description of Frenside places much more emphasis on the critic's own dissatisfaction with his abilities but he does express his disappointment straightforwardly. Through Frenside Wharton is moving towards the depiction of Berry as a willing and able literary adviser; as she depicts it, his renunciation of all thought of being an artist is the sensible, self-aware action of the man who recognises his own limitations.

Wharton first met Berry in the summer of 1883, when she was twenty-one, and on holiday at Bar Harbor. She immediately felt him to be someone with whom she could have a completely rounded relationship: 'We had seen a great deal of each other for a few weeks, and the encounter had given me a fleeting hint of what the communication of kindred intelligences might be',[28] but he failed to speak and passed out of her life until 1897 when they renewed a friendship which was to endure until his death in 1927. The portrait of Berry in the autobiography gives no other hint of the disappointment which was always to colour her attitude towards him; his sexual preferences were always for silly, pretty women – on neither of which count Edith Wharton qualified – and he never seemed to feel the need to make any enduring emotional commitment.

Berry actually failed Wharton in ways which related to her sexual self-esteem and therefore when seeking to enhance his rôle in her life story she needed to delineate and contiguously increase in value the most satisfactory side of their relationship – that which was concerned with her art. The idea that her intellectual and creative talents might be the very cause of his failure to commit himself to her more fully is explored by Wharton through the relationships between artist and critic in the fiction where she controls and distances her emotional disappointment by various means, not least of which is the writing of the artist as a man. From the jealousy which destroys the friendship between Levick and Richard Thaxter, through the resigned support which Frenside offers to Vance Weston, to the portrait of Walter Berry as intellectual midwife to her early fictional offspring, she charts the passage of the critic from personal disappointment to a state of something like contentment with his own particular gifts. In enhancing the rôle of Berry as critic and mentor Wharton is able to show obliquely just how much he esteems her because the one thing which he gives her wholeheartedly and unequivocally is the one thing that is likely to cause him the pain of envy or self-doubt. His self-sacrifice has made her artistic achievement possible.

There is, however, in the fiction, a reminder of the unfulfilled and sorrowful side to the Wharton/Berry relationship, although here Berry's attitudes are demonstrated by Richard and Vance rather than by Levick and Frenside. Both writers find sensitive, cultured, intelligent women, their equals, if not their superiors, in understanding – Rose Lansing in 'Literature' and Halo Tarrant in *The Gods Arrive* – who are willing to commit themselves to the men and their work. In each case the woman is badly hurt and disillusioned when the artist is drawn into an affair with a beautiful but frivolous socialite: Richard with the pneumatically entitled Carmen Bliss, and Vance with Floss Delaney. Both men ultimately prefer their soul rather than their bed mates but the terrible misery which is caused by the male rejection of the female of intelligence and sympathy is cogently expressed in both stories. In the fiction Wharton was able to give a voice to the pain and frustration which she had to conquer in the all-affirming drive of *A Backward Glance*.

The recounting of childhood experiences dominates both the unfinished autobiography and the fully written part of 'Literature'. That Wharton considered her early years to have been crucial to her creative development is evidenced again and again by the writing and re-writing of her memories of first things and the picture she builds up of the beginnings of the artistic impulse. 'Literature' and 'Life and I' represent the lower layers of the 'palimpsest' which is the self-portrait of the artist, the autobiographical impulse being much less straightforwardly enacted in *Hudson River Bracketed* and *The Gods Arrive* where Wharton does not depict Vance's early years, significant revelations of language and feeling coming to him much later than to Richard Thaxter or to Edith herself. Autobiography asserts a sense of tradition between past and present selves and the repeated writing-out of her childhood is her way of imposing an order upon the confusion which the child – Richard or Edith – expresses as a longing for a more structured existence. As she says in 'Life and I':

Next came Coleridge's 'Friend'. Let no one ask me why! I can only suppose it answered to some hidden need to order my thoughts, and get things into some kind of logical relation to each other: a need which developed in me almost as early as the desire to be kissed and thought pretty! It originated, perhaps, in the sense that weighed on my whole childhood – the sense of bewilderment, of the need of guidance, the longing to understand *what it was all about*. My little corner of the cosmos seemed like a dark trackless region 'where ignorant armies clash by night', and I was oppressed by the sense that I was too small and ignorant and alone ever to find my way about in it. . . .[29]

She talks repeatedly of her intellectual and even emotional isolation among her family and peers but the writing is inevitably coloured by her adult sense of what that isolation means. In 'Literature', however, Wharton is able to use Richard Thaxter as a surrogate, giving her the opportunity to explore her experiences through another and also to see how her life looks on a page which does not declare itself to be autobiography. The text is, by this translation, subject to a radically different type of scrutiny from the reader. There are many direct correlations between 'Literature' and 'Life and I'; from the first kiss, received in the autobiography, given in 'Literature', through the 'making up' of stories in childhood and the form which the creative frenzy took, to the first attempt at a piece of literary criticism, the texts run parallel. The central difference between the two is the degree of adult interference in the reporting, the fiction is left to speak for itself whilst the autobiography is subject to mature interpretation, though not in the same prescriptive form as in *A Backward Glance*.

An important correlation between 'Literature' and 'Life and I' is in the manner of presentation of the child's relationship with her/his father who, in both cases, is singled out as the one person who might be capable of lighting the darkness for his child but is prevented by other members of the family from doing so. To work back through the palimpsest, in *A Backward Glance* Edith's father is described in the language of unfulfilled potential which also characterises the portraits of Lodge, Winthrop and the others:

The new Tennysonian rhythms also moved my father greatly; and I imagine there was a time when his rather rudimentary love of verse might have been developed had he had anyone with whom to share it. But my mother's matter-of-factness must have shrivelled up any such buds of fancy; and in later years I remember his reading only Macaulay, Prescott, Washington Irving, and every book of travel he could find. Arctic explorations especially absorbed him, and I have wondered since what stifled cravings had once germinated in him, and what manner of man he was really meant to be. That he was a lonely one, haunted by something always unexpressed and unattained, I am sure.[30]

It is in her father and his 'rather rudimentary' literary instincts that Wharton seeks the origins of her own artistic impulse. The language of possibility is placed up against the known fact of the hard indifference of her mother to the life of the imagination. As Lucretia Jones 'must have' crushed the artistic leanings of her husband so that he never achieved his potential, so his daughter's portrait of him as frozen by tales of arctic voyages is freighted with the inadequacy of what he actually was.

In the earlier autobiography, 'Life and I', Wharton presents her father more positively, in terms of the little he was able to do for her: 'My father, who had a vague enjoyment in "sight-seeing", unaccompanied by any artistic or intellectual curiosity, or any sense of the relations of things to each other, was delighted to take me about, and with our Ruskin in hand we explored every corner of Florence and Venice'.[31] The description of father and daughter as tourists is prefaced by an acknowledgement of his passivity and ignorance, but although he is not a guide in Wharton's constant search for a sense of tradition, expressed here as 'the relation of things to each other', he is a courtly, obliging escort. The picture of her father in 'Life and I', notwithstanding his inadequacy, goes some way towards satisfying her constant urge toward the explanation of the fact of her creative abilities; his sympathy can at least be viewed as a mild form of encouragement, as an acknowledgement of the importance of her interests. The picture of her father in her autobiographies remains, however, vague; the prevailing tone of *A Backward Glance* is so determinedly uncontentious that it is impossible for Wharton to present specific ideas or examples of her mother's repressive influence on her father and the brevity of 'Life and I' on the subject also means that her theories about 'what manner of man he was really meant to be' remain undeveloped. In 'Literature', however, she is unconstrained by history or the need for autobiographical discretion and so her portrait of the Reverend Thaxter is more fully drawn and has much of interest to say about her own father.

Richard Thaxter is given the same longings as Edith Wharton herself for a structure to his education and for a guide 'to supply the links'[32] between things. The incapacity of the Reverend Thaxter to be that guide is fully explained in 'Literature', and it is most tellingly evidenced by the utterly debilitating effect of his having been misguided in his choice of career. That the Reverend Thaxter has lost his faith and cannot live with himself in the church or with his family outside it, becomes gradually evident to Richard and helps him, later, to come to terms with his father's failure of communication. As Wharton covers her own father's inadequacies with generous conjecture about the constraints of his lifestyle so Richard is able to focus on the exhaustion produced by both the parish, which seemed to the boy to be 'like a helpless cantankerous old relative for whose welfare everyone was actively concerned and who met every effort on her behalf with fresh complaints and demands',[33] and the struggle involved in keeping up the pretence of faith. However, his father is at least responsible, as the opening line of the novel declares, for the 'most decisive event of Richard Thaxter's life'.[34] Just as Wharton remembers her father's reading of *The Lays of Ancient Rome* as an awakening to the power of poetic language, so the Reverend Thaxter provides the catalyst to the early development of his son's linguistic awareness. The discovery of the sound of words in rhythmic combination is the single most important event in the lives of both children, the numinous quality of the discovery being made literal in Richard's case by both the setting and the actual poetry:

> Thus immersed in beautitude, Dick was nevertheless aware of the progress of the service as a burrowing animal may be of the passage of the daylight overhead. Some obscure sense of the lapse of time told him when to lower his legs for a hymn, and enabled him to distinguish the gospel and epistle from the lessons; and he always knew when he could abandon himself to the final repose of the sermon. He was sure, therefore, that the sermon had begun, and had been several minutes in progress, before the thing happened which, even there, on the spot, he obscurely felt to be a great event, an event as great as could happen in anything so small as himself.
>
> 'Oh my son Absalom, my son, my son Absalom, would God I had died for thee, Oh Absalom, my son, my son!'
>
> That was what happened – this rain of celestial syllables pouring down on him from heights higher than the swallow's nest and the summer sky ... he didn't care a straw what the words meant: that had nothing to do with it. He simply noticed they *were* words; and that was the great event. He had noticed many things already: birds, dogs, beetles, tadpoles, people's faces, the look of rooms and the pictures on their walls. But he had never noticed words, or the sound of words joined together;

and now the wonder of the linked syllables seemed to catch his little heart in a grasp of fire.[35]

That it should be the father, earthly or celestial, who is responsible for initiating the love of language in his child, the 'sensuous rapture produced by the sound and sight of the words',[36] as she describes it in 'Life and I', is Wharton's tribute to her own sad parent. In the fiction she is able to communicate a sense of how such an 'event' can be a determining factor in the future growth and development of a person because she can overstate the case. The description of any such singular occasion in her own child-hood would inevitably have been subject to interference from her mature autobiographical standpoint and her readers' preconceptions of the genre, whereas she can write Richard's feelings straight onto the page without demur. The 'event' for the child is the effect of the order of language, the combination and rhythm exclusive of meaning which distinguishes the lament from the diurnal repetitions of household talk. The substance of life is changed by Richard's inner response to the words; the significance of the sound, not the sense, is what is revelatory. The effect is entirely aural, as Wharton makes plain by Richard's later efforts to reproduce the words: '"o my so nabsalan my son my so nabsalan, wood god" (There were wood-gods in his fairy books, so he understood that)'[37] and he refuses to listen when his grandmother tries to tell him the story behind the words. The experience makes the child aware of both the creative and the imitable power of language; it is in him to repeat the words, to annex them for his own satisfaction, and he can also build upon them a whole new personal mythology as Wharton did herself, according to 'Life and I':

From that moment I was enthralled by *words*. It mattered very little whether I understood them or not: the sound was the essential thing. Wherever I went they sang to me like the birds in an enchanted forest. And they had *looks* as well as sound: each one had its own gestures and physiognomy ...

When I read my first poetry I felt that 'bliss was it in that dawn to be alive'. Here were words transfigured, lifted from earth to heaven! I think my first experience of rhyme was the hearing of the *Lays of Ancient Rome* read aloud by my father. The movement of the metre was intoxicating: I can still feel the thump thump of my little heart as I listened to it! ... But this increase of knowledge was as nought compared to the sensuous rapture produced by the sound and sight of the words. I never for a moment ceased to be conscious of them. They were visible, almost tangible presences, with faces as distinct as those of the persons among whom I lived.[38]

Having had the gift of poetry bestowed upon them by the father, both children then proceed sequentially to the printed page for inspiration. Access to a seemingly unlimited supply of words has allowed them to be a part of an ulterior world and, with the freedom this brings, they then move towards establishing themselves as a part of a pattern, of a larger tradition, as they do both in and through the process of 'making up', where they invent their own stories.

There is little to choose between Wharton's autobiographical account of 'making up' in 'Life and I' and her fictional account in 'Literature', so closely do they correlate. Both children invent their own stories as they hold a book open, turning pages at the appropriate moment and moving up and down the room as they read/invent. They have been driven toward the printed page by a double act of cognition: that the inspiration for the printed word is the imagination and that the printed word can be a source of inspiration to the imagination. In the retelling of this childhood 'ritual' Wharton is not only chronicling the development of her creative instincts but also locating them in the context of a larger literary tradition. The association between invention and the text is both a stimulus to the imagination and an insistent precedent for 'the act of fiction'. Linguistic potential is understood to lie in the established printed word, the awakening to the sound of poetry leading directly to the page even though meaning is still of no importance. The use of the book is a movement towards trying to establish for herself, and for Richard, a sense of continuity, to discover 'the relations of things to each other':

I did not want to *tell* the stories I was forever inventing, I wanted to *read them aloud*; and every day for hours paced the nursery floor, engaged in the absorbing occupation of reading these inexhaustible tales from a book, which, as often as not, I held upside-down, but of which I never failed to turn the pages. This strange pursuit was called 'making-up', and was carried on long after I learned to read, and always book in hand ... I would be shut up in [my mother's] bedroom, and measuring its floor with rapid strides, while I poured out to my tattered Tauchnitz the accumulated floods of my pent-up eloquence. Oh, the exquisite relief of those moments of escape from the effort of trying to 'be like other children'! The rapture of finding myself in my own rich world of dreams! I don't think I exaggerate or embellish in retrospect the ecstasy which transported my little body and soul when I shut myself in and caught up my precious Tauchnitz.[39]

The only significant respect in which her account of her own 'making up' differs from her account of the process in 'Literature' is in the claim she makes for the status of the child's invented text. For Richard: 'The story, as he walked, grew out of the book, seemed to curl up from it in a sort of silvery mist; he had to turn the pages as he would have done if he had really been reading what was printed on them. And his own story, somehow, *was* printed on them while he read: it overlay the other like a palimpsest'.[40] The symbolic value of this, communicable only in the fictionalised account, is in the expression it gives to the notion of precedence, the development of the child's awareness that there is a tradition both to draw upon and to add to in the personal act of invention; the grasping of the prior text gives the children a sense of 'the relation of things to each other' that they have both been searching for. The motion which is built into the creative process – Wharton strode around her mother's bedroom and the excitement of invention for Richard is actually reflected in the pace of his physical movements – gives an indication of the kinaesthetic totality of the process. Wharton engages completely with the experience of the child; in both cases she describes their telling of the tale as 'reading': the act of turning the pages, of sustaining the myth that their own story exists in a tangible form outside the imagination, is the primary and necessary fiction which must be accepted before the actual 'making-up' can take place. The creative act requires a structure of presentation before its 'rich world of dreams' can be penetrated. Wharton describes Richard as feeling 'the fiery laurels on his brow',[41] as she places him – not without ironic intent – firmly into a literary tradition which is both actual and metaphorical. In the 'Literature' fragment Wharton describes the tale as being directly generated from the text; as with the linguistic revelations of the Reverend Thaxter's Absalom sermon, so the fictionalised version of 'making-up' can be presented as numinous or other-worldly. She can describe the first creative acts of the imagined artist in a quasi-mystical light – the 'silvery mist' – because the restraints built into the act of autobiography do not apply. She is able here to give full expression to the sense of wonder and reverence which the memory of her own childhood's bardic impulses still inspires.

The fact that in the exercise of the imagination the child draws in 'the printed inventions of others'[42] is one of the methods, in the early autobiographical work, by which Wharton attempts to allevi-ate her feelings of cultural deprivation. The absence of a sense of 'the relation of things to each other'[43] or, as she describes it in 'Literature', the child's longings for 'formulas to compel'[44] his words, communicates a need for both form and context. The urge towards a larger patterning and structuring of individual experi-ence is the message of the autobiographical writing as well as its source of imagery. The vaunted purpose of *A Backward Glance* is to recapture the 'pathetic picturesqueness' of the old order of New York, to retrieve, in an archaeological version of the 'palimpsest', the place which now exists only in her memory 'as much a vanished city as Atlantis or the lowest layer of Schliemann's Troy'.[45] As it was in the earlier writing the authorial impulsion is the search for and imposition of a form which will satisfy Whar-ton's lifelong preoccupation with her historical and topographical place as a writer.

Her final fictional expression of the search for such a sense of continuity takes for its subject the artist struggling for aesthetic enlightenment, showing the progress of his education, first in east coast America and then in Europe, working against the current of his upbringing in the relentlessly renewable mid-west. The task, however, proves too great for Wharton; she sets her writer, Vance Weston, too many difficulties to overcome and he ends, as do so many of her male characters, as merely insufficient, and certainly insufficient to carry the weight of authorial investment in the subject of what makes an artist.

In the notebook plan of *Hudson River Bracketed* Wharton sub-divides the text into seven separate books – 'Dawn, Daylight, Morning, Noon, Afternoon, Evening, Dawn' – signifying the developmental but also ineluctable nature of Vance's progress. The design of this overview, however, is not reflected in the completed novel, the work falling victim to its own purpose. That purpose, to tell the story of the post-war novelist, located in an exaggeratedly deprived mid-west, fails when the character and situation cannot bear the weight of the primarily autobiographical motivation of the writing. The assumptions of the Vance Weston novels – in their movement away from the traditions and trappings of a society which, although lacking a coherent aesthetic, provided the means of access to a wider culture for Edith Wharton and Richard Thaxter – continually undercut the intended development of the narrative. In the outline of the novel which she sent to Appleton, her publishers, she concludes by saying:

> I want to try to draw the experiences of an unusually intelligent modern American youth, of average education and situation, on whom the great revelation of the Past, which everything in modern American training tends to exclude, or at least to minimize, rushes in through the million channels of art, of history, and of human beings of another civilisation.
>
> I cannot give more details yet. But the canvas will be broad and full of figures. Vance Weston becomes a writer – literary critic and novelist – and dies young, full of awe of the world's wonder and beauty.[46]

The chief problem for Wharton in attempting to carry out this plan is that so many of the revelations, the experiences, with which she seeks to endow her central character conflict convulsively with her notion of the possibilities for the young man of 'average education and situation', and the mode of expression in the novel is often as crude and simple as her first projection of her aims. The claim she makes throughout the published autobiography for her singularity is actually validated through her portrait of Vance, though not in the sense she intended; part of that singularity being owed to the fact of having spent most of one's childhood in the capital cities of Europe, inheriting the use of a 'gentleman's library', and living in a community where behaviour was based on 'nearly three hundred years of social observance: the concerted living up to long-established standards of honour and conduct, of education and manners'.[47] So, expressed simply, the special conditions of Wharton's background do not translate, in their effects, into the life of Vance Weston. In the writing of the two novels, *Hudson River Bracketed* and *The Gods Arrive*, she is moving one step further in the portrayal of deprivation; to depict a known quantity, a Bay Lodge, in Vance's stead would have contradicted her oft-repeated conviction that the artist cannot be nurtured into creativity. However, she over-reaches her capacity to translate the experiences of her own development into another's more disadvantaged existence through the confusion of her desire to give empirical proof of her belief in the 'unpampered vocation' with her by now hardened prejudices against 'everything in modern American training'.

Whatever else, though, it should be borne in mind when reading *Hudson River Bracketed* that Wharton told the editor-in-chief at Appleton's: 'I am sure it is my best book'[48] and included both Vance Weston stories on her own short list of her five most preferred works. Despite the almost inevitable failure to live up to the agenda she had set for herself in the writing, she invited judgement on her whole artistic achievement from the basis of these novels. Their significance for her personally – in autobiographical and topographical terms – is ultimately of more importance than the fact that her ideas are not sustained by either prose or protagonist.

The novels follow Vance from Euphoria, Illinois, to New York and from there to Europe in pursuit of an aesthetic education. He makes an unfortunate marriage with his cousin, Laura Lou Tracy, but she obligingly fulfils the promise of the fragility which is her main attraction, and dies, freeing him to enter into a relationship with Halo Tarrant, who leaves her husband for him. He meets Halo early in the story and indeed she is responsible for introducing him to a whole range of experiences and possibilities by allowing him access to the house, the Willows, from which the novel derives its title, Hudson River Bracketed being a nineteenth-century American architectural style. The Willows is the property of an eccentric cousin of Halo's family and is maintained as a sort of shrine to the lifestyle of its last occupant, Miss Emily Lorburn, a relic of nineteenth-century gentility whose library offers to Vance the life-changing opportunity of reading Coleridge, Marlowe, Marvell and others – all those authors, in fact, to whom the young Edith Jones, being forbidden novels, had free access. Thus inspired, Vance writes 'Instead', a novel which commemorates Emily Lorburn and her way of life, and wins great public praise and attention before turning his attention to a novel about present-day New York. *Hudson River Bracketed* ends with Vance and Halo together, not in triumph but in the full consciousness of the suffering which has been caused to all involved in their previous relationships and the effect which such beginnings must have on their future.

The Gods Arrive opens with their departure from America as they travel together to Europe, unwed but initially strong enough in their feelings for one another to brazen out the inevitable disadvantages of such an arrangement. However, the disadvantages soon become apparent, and even overwhelming, and they all fall upon Halo, whose position is made worse by her husband's refusal to divorce her. Vance is fêted all over Europe as the writer of the hour and Halo is forbidden access, as his mistress, to the circles in which he is lionised. In spite of this she and Vance try to live both together and apart in a variety of European countries but it is the fact of Vance's infidelity to Halo with Floss Delaney that nearly finishes everything between them. It is only when Vance is finally able to throw off his infatuation with Floss and, through the good offices of St Augustine, whose *Confessions* bring him through a life crisis, that he can return to Halo with some consciousness of the nature of relationship and the commitment which is required of him. Halo is pregnant with their child but has not told him about her condition so as to leave him free to marry Floss if he wants to. The novel nevertheless ends with their reunion and his obeisance to the visible fact of her motherhood:

> 'You see we belong to each other after all,' she said; but as her arms sank about his neck he bent his head and put his lips to a fold of her loose dress.[49]

They come together at the close of this novel as they did at the end of the first, older, wiser, sadder, and forced to be content, as innumerable Wharton characters before them have been forced to be content, with life on a lower level of intensity and fulfilment.

In many ways the characterisation of Halo Tarrant is the most successful and coherent feature of the two novels; the very nature of her background and social position make her more personally accessible to the author than Vance, whose posited origins interfere with the transplantation of Wharton's self-referential ideas about the growth of the artist into the story of his life. This is not to say that all Wharton's work is dependent for its success on the degree of personal involvement she felt with the characters or text in general but in the case of her portraits of the artist the autobiographical impulse is crucial and it is upon this that the novels turn. That the next book she worked on after *The Gods Arrive* was *A Backward Glance* shows her continuing in the autobiographical mode rather than coming into it anew, and the struggle she had to keep on course with her plan to depict the triumph of the creative gift in spite of 'everything in modern American training' partly accounts for the stiffly reverential tones of the official 'life'.

The Vance Weston novels suffer from Wharton's failure to interweave the theory which underlies them with the narrative so that the most interesting feature of the stories soon becomes the fact that she articulates so many of her personal, social and artistic tenets through the various mouthpieces of George Frenside, Halo Tarrant and Vance himself. The sense of the past, nurtured in her own case by the extensive European travel which her family undertook when she was a child, 'that background of beauty and old-established order',[50] has to be located elsewhere for Vance and whilst she sets out with the intention of making the foundation of his aesthetic development the house, the Willows, from which the first book takes its title, she cannot remain serious about her original intent. She overdetermines the house as a symbol of the past and its treasures for Vance, and expects the mere fact of its existence to do all the work for her whilst she constantly undercuts its intended importance with the carelessness of her prose:

> Under his touch the familiar setting of the Willows became steeped in poetry. It was his embodiment of the Past: that strange and overwhelming element had entered into his imagination in the guise of these funny turrets and balconies, turgid upholsteries and dangling crystals. Suddenly lifted out of a boundless contiguity of Euphorias, his mind struck root deep down in accumulated layers of experience, in centuries of struggle, passion and aspiration – so that this absurd house, the joke of Halo's childhood, was to him the very emblem of man's long effort, was Chartres, the Parthenon, the Pyramids.[51]

The language which strains after significance in seeking to communicate the dawning of a sense of the past in Vance's consciousness is not allowed to make a serious impression before the adjectival onslaught of the throwaway 'funny', 'turgid', 'dangling', 'absurd' renders it impotent. The contrast, instead of surprising and enlightening the reader with the simplicity of the cultural phenomenon which has acted as catalyst to Vance's aesthetic awakening, is self-defeating; the more she emphasises the ridicu-

lous aspects of the house and its meaning to him the less
convincing Wharton becomes: 'The mere discovery that there were
people who had been born and died in the same house was
romance and poetry to Vance'.[52] It is not, however, enough merely
to tell us this if we cannot be made to understand it through the
precise use of topographical enlightenment which is the disting-
uishing mark of her best work.

The language is weary and simplistic and even the image of
precedence, of discovery as well as invention, the 'palimpsest' of
her own and Richard Thaxter's experience, has dwindled to
'accumulated layers'. The excitement of the discovery and the
growth of a sense of tradition has been dissipated in the proselytis-
ing strain which also comes between author and reader in *A
Backward Glance*. This is not only evident in her use of images,
however, but more directly in her narrow linguistic intentions; the
Willows is presented unequivocally as an 'embodiment' which is
'ripe with meaning',[53] Wharton leaving us no alternative but to see
its importance as the equal of 'Chartres, the Parthenon, the
Pyramids'. This verbal prescription of audience reaction is a late
autobiographical mannerism and not one which transfers appropri-
ately to the fiction. The easy qualitative superlatives are left to
carry the burden of seemingly limitless and ultimately meaningless
signification: 'overwhelming', 'boundless', 'deep down', 'extraor-
dinary' and 'countless', even the echo and deliberate refutation of
the idea of continuity contained within the use of 'contiguity' is
dissipated by the carelessness of the language which surrounds it.

The most moving aspect of the novels – particularly *The Gods
Arrive* – and that which concentrates the author's mind most
effectively is the writing on the subject of marriage and relationships conducted both within and without its orbit. Vance's first
marriage, to the inarticulate Laura Lou, soon becomes a prison of
arrested communication for them both as they have no common
language except that of the body: 'Pressed each to each, they clung
fast, groping for one another through the troubled channels of the
blood'.[54] Halo's relationship with her husband, Lewis Tarrant, on
the other hand, suffers from too close a scrutiny of linguistic intent:

> 'Oh, Lewis, you've discovered a great novelist!' She prided
> herself on the tactfulness of the formula; but enthusiasm for
> others was apt to excite her husband's suspicions, even when it
> implied praise for himself. . . . Adroitly as she had canalized her

enthusiasm, she did not expect an immediate response. She knew that what she had said must first be transposed and become his own.[55]

There is a complex equation of intention and signification being documented here in contrast to the most basic form of communication by which Vance and Laura Lou partially understand each other. Halo must frame her response so that it is – contradictorily – both subdued and infectious, otherwise Lewis cannot annex it for his own use and still retain the sense of superiority which is so vital to the equilibrium of their marriage. Halo leaves the room as her husband delivers his verdict on Vance's story as 'it would be easier for Lewis to get through with the business of appropriating her opinions if she stayed out of hearing while he was doing it'.[56] She is given voice only through him and so must organise her reactions to take account of her limited opportunities for effective speech.

In contrast to these two negative portraits, however, is the configuration of an understanding of the marriage bond in *The Gods Arrive* as the key which is missing from the life of the artist, a significant part of Vance's emotional and creative immaturity deriving from his attitude to women: 'Intellectual comradeship between lovers was unattainable; that was not the service women could render to men'.[57] Wharton repeatedly emphasises the liberating effect of commitment – of the brain as well as the heart – which, despite Vance's churlish rejection of the dual possibilities which life with Halo offers, is eventually realised here. Like Fulvia Vivaldi in Wharton's first novel, *The Valley of Decision*, Halo is stronger than the man to whom she expects to act as intellectual and emotional handmaiden and whilst Vance gropes towards an understanding of what marriage is – 'an emanation of the will of man'[58] – Halo has known all along:

Why should she and Vance not marry and take their chance with other ordinary people? They might have a child, and then there would be something about which to build the frame-work. They would become a nucleus, their contradictory cravings would meet in a common purpose, their being together and belonging to each other would acquire a natural meaning.[59]

She sees the formalisation of their relationship as endowing an organic validity, the biological imperative reconciling their differences and bestowing an order applicable not merely to their situation but to the situation of the species. Wharton, in perpetual search for 'formulas to compel' her words, her deeds, her emotions, endows a sanctity upon marriage in this, her last complete novel, giving it the capacity to act as healer of wounds and to communicate a sense of the possibilities for human relationship in a form more sustaining and enduring than any other social structure.

The two Vance Weston novels and the formal autobiography are determinedly finished texts; the retrospective framing of events with present experience shows Edith Wharton to have given up the interest and excitement in process which directs the writing in both 'Literature' and 'Life and I'. *A Backward Glance*, with all its reticences of tone and content is the final layer on the autobiographical palimpsest and only the occasional crack or thinness in the daub lets us glimpse the emotions which still lie behind the narrative portrait. *A Backward Glance* displays a straining towards completion and the same urge for conclusiveness unfortunately directs the fiction, curtailing much of its imaginative and linguistic potential. The discursive method so much a feature of 'Literature', where the transposition of her own experience into the life of Richard Thaxter is concerned with the multitudinous possibilities of language, has been abandoned in favour of the mode of opinion. At the end of *The Gods Arrive* Wharton causes Vance to reach the point of self-revelation which facilitates his reconciliation with Halo through his discovery of the writing of self in *The Confessions of St Augustine*. The authorial intent behind this is double, the light of formal autobiographical patterning is thrown back over the events of Vance's past, and the words of the model autobiographer effect both the closure of the novel and a significant development in the artist himself:

'And Thou didst beat back my weak sight, dazzling me with Thy splendour, and I perceived that I was far from Thee, in the land of unlikeness, and I heard Thy voice crying to me: "I am the Food of the full-grown. Become a man and thou shalt feed on Me."'

The Food of the full-grown – of the full-grown! That was the key to his grandmother's last words. 'Become a man and thou shalt feed on Me' was the message of experience to the soul; and what was youth but the Land of Unlikeness?[60]

The language of St Augustine provides a sanction for the finite language of the novels – and only faith could provide such certainty. The processes of doubt and failure in its attainment make the certainty all the more valuable and incontrovertible. The autobiographical act is made to carry the burden of completion, the summation and endowment of mature significance upon the events and texts of the past.

The point at which I began, Wharton's disclaimer: 'my life has been too uneventful to be worth recording. Indeed I had never even thought of recording it for my own amusement' is refuted by the repeated testing and working through of her perceptions of her past self, its relationships and topography, in her writings. Whilst the early texts explore that past, the dominating mood of hindsight and conviction prevents any such investigation from taking place in the finished works, a mood which does not, fortunately, infect the writing of her American historical novels, the last group of texts to be discussed in this book. The society of *The Age of Innocence* (1920), *Old New York* (1924), and *The Buccaneers* (1938), comes under scrutiny with all the radical clarity of her highest art.

7
The Age of Innocence

Beginning in 1920 Wharton wrote a number of historical novels all set in the American nineteenth century. *The Age of Innocence*, published in that year, opens in the early 1870s; the four novellas of the *Old New York* series, published collectively in 1924, have the decades of their setting as sub-titles: *False Dawn* (The 'forties), *The Old Maid*, (The 'fifties), *The Spark* (The 'sixties), and *New Year's Day* (The 'seventies); and *The Buccaneers*, Wharton's last and unfinished novel, published posthumously in 1938, is also set in the early 1870s.

In a letter to Bernard Berenson, written during the composition of *The Age of Innocence*, Wharton outlined her views on the possibilities for fiction in the post-war world, given here by her biographer, R. W. B. Lewis, in Berenson's paraphrase of her words:

> Before the war you could write fiction without indicating the period, the present being assumed. The war has put an end to that for a long time, and everything will soon have to be timed with reference to it. In other words, the historical novel with all its vices will be the only possible form for fiction.[1]

The war did indeed make it 'possible' for Wharton to write an American historical novel, to frame her society in terms of its past, because the history of her country was the only certainty left for her to 'assume'. This is not merely a negative act, however, nor even a making-do, but a positive re-adjustment to the differences made by the war to both the American and European conscious-ness of their joint and separate histories. When Yvor Winters, in his 1938 essay, 'Maule's Curse', described the work of Fenimore Cooper in *Satanstoe*, *The Chainbearer* and *The Pioneers* 'as a prelude to such work by Mrs. Wharton as the four novelettes of the *Old New York* series and *The Age of Innocence*',[2] he was talking about the establishment of a tradition of American historicising. Where Fenimore Cooper writes in order to foster a sense of the past, to invent a background for the new novel of American manners, Wharton writes to commemorate a past which has been superseded by the cataclysmic social upheavals of the war years. The pre-history of the post-war world is American as well as European, and at last there is a shared sense of the past – both topographic and historic – between continents, which can find expression in Wharton's fiction.

In her historical novels Wharton describes, whilst writing specifically of New York, the community of cultural and social structures and pursuits between Europe and America. In *A Backward Glance*, when describing her relationship with Henry James she says:

> The truth is that he belonged irrevocably to the old America out of which I also came, and of which – almost – it might paradoxically be said that to follow up its last traces one had to come to Europe; as I discovered when my French and English friends told me, on reading *The Age of Innocence*, that they had no idea New York life in the 'seventies had been so like that of the English cathedral town, or the French *ville de province*, of the same date.[3]

Where Cooper had to make explicit the rapidity with which his society was developing: 'Five years had wrought greater changes than a century would produce in countries where time and labor have given permanency to the works of man'[4] in order to give it credibility as a culture, Wharton could express – precisely and effectively – the New York of the 1870s in social anthropological terms, and thereby endow historical dignity. A bald statement, such as that by Cooper, of the American spatio-time compression of history is no longer necessary, the 'tribal'[5] structures of Wharton's childhood New York have been made authentic by their passing and consequent relegation to the museum. As she writes in an essay 'A Little Girl's New York', published in *Harper's Magazine* in March 1938: 'Everything that used to form the fabric of our daily life has been torn in shreds, trampled on, destroyed; and hundreds of little incidents, habits, traditions which, when I began to record my past, seemed too insignificant to set down, have acquired the historical importance of fragments of dress and furniture dug up in a Babylonian tomb'.[6]

Odo Valsecca's reconstruction of the Italian past in his archaeological adventures in Naples can now be equalled by the American myth-maker. Wharton entitles her quartet of stories *Old New York*, the internal temporal contradiction finally equalising 'Old' and 'New' worlds in terms of history. The writing of the historical novel from an American perspective at last sanctions Wharton's freedom of movement between cultures. It is, however, ironic that the benefits of this freedom and its attendant sense of personal and national historical certainty can only be articulated by the artist in the process of registering its loss.

The Age of Innocence is set during the declining years of the nineteenth century, three decades which, according to Wharton, were to see more social upheaval than the preceding three centuries, and, when added to the war years, were to change the western world out of all recognition. To turn again to *A Backward Glance*: 'Between the point of view of my Huguenot great-great-grandfather, who came from the French Palatinate to participate in the founding of New Rochelle, and my own father, who died in 1882, there were fewer differences than between my father and the post-war generation of Americans'.[7] The manner of the resolution of the moral dilemma at the heart of the novel reflects the old order, Wharton making Newland Archer's reaffirmation of his commitment to his wife and 'tribe' seem almost the final act of the nineteenth century. The story concerns the love which develops between Newland and his wife's cousin, the unhappily married Countess Ellen Olenska, and the way in which these would-be lovers and their network of New York families deal with the situation. The points of reference of the novel, its landscape, its characters, are those of Edith Wharton's childhood. The New York which she sought to celebrate and memorialise in her formal autobiography is better served by *The Age of Innocence*: the city and its values are the only victors in this story, but their expectations are here fulfilled for the last time.

Within Edith Wharton's historical novels the concerns which she explored in the fiction and the guidebooks through an alien topography come to fruition. The society of *The Age of Innocence* becomes what Italy once was for the novitiate writer and the tropes with which Wharton illuminates Newland Archer's sentimental growth seem deliberately to invoke *The Valley of Decision* in the achievement of their effects; for instance:

The Marchioness's foolish lisp had called up a vision of the little fire-lit drawing-room and the sound of the carriage-wheels returning down the deserted street. He thought of a story he had read, of some peasant children in Tuscany lighting a bunch of straw in a wayside cavern, and revealing old silent images in their painted tomb. . . .[8]

Wharton's view of the Italian scene, as expressed in her travel-books and in her first novel, is marked by an uneasy mixture of the wish to illuminate the present with images from the past and an antipathy towards a museum-culture which esteems acquisition above understanding. This ambivalence continues to colour her writing in *The Age of Innocence*. The most revered relics in New York society in *The Age of Innocence* are actually the van der Luydens, Henry and Louisa, influential only because 'they make themselves so rare';[9] their value inheres in their obsolescence. The 'large shrouded room . . . so complete an image of its owners' encases them in 'the airless atmosphere of a perfectly irreproachable existence',[10] and, as they cultivate the atmosphere of the tomb, so they are actually responsible for their own relegation to the museum and the larger growth of a museum-culture. Their values become as superannuated as their habits and their surroundings. The mere fact of the existence of these values, rather than understanding of the principles upon which they are based, has been mistakenly deemed sufficient to ensure their survival.

Wharton uses the museum in the park in *The Age of Innocence* in two ways: firstly, as the writer of the historical novel, to pinpoint the specific stage of development of the city of New York – as Newland Archer says: 'Some day, I suppose, it will be a great Museum' – and secondly to show how the place and its people are subject to the inexorably levelling force of time. The museum is the only possible location for the last meeting which Ellen Olenska and Newland Archer have alone together, there being 'no churches . . . no monuments' to reduce them to the necessary level of anonymity elsewhere in the city, and it forces them to a realisation of their own inconsequence:

Presently he rose and approached the case before which she stood. Its glass shelves were crowded with small broken objects – hardly recognizable domestic utensils, of discolored bronze and other time-blurred substances.

'It seems cruel,' she said, 'that after a while nothing matters . . .

any more than these little things, that used to be necessary and important to forgotten people, and now have to be guessed at under a magnifying glass and labeled: "Use unknown." '[11]

The museum strips from them all relationship except the one which speaks of their ultimate irrelevance – their relationship with history. Their lives, when removed from their social context, from the interaction with people and things which endows meaning upon the individual existence, are as meaningless as the 'small broken objects' once in daily use, whose purpose has been lost and whose sole value lies in their age and consequent mysteriousness. Newland's desperate attempt to deny his relatedness, his topography: '"I want – I want somehow to get away with you into a world where words like that – categories like that – won't exist. Where we shall be simply two human beings who love each other, who are the whole of life to each other; and nothing else will matter"', is doomed, as Ellen knows: '"Oh, my dear – where is that country? Have you ever been there?"'[12] Individuals are not separable from their time and place; if they were to be so then they would be devoid of all referents and as irrelevant to the business of living as the objects in the museum.

The social customs and practices of the Faubourg which so mystified John Durham in *Madame de Treymes* are now shown to have their equivalent in nineteenth-century New York; the boundaries are clearly defined, if not publicly acknowledged, although this is only possible because Wharton has chosen to memorialise the historical moment of her youth. The tribal structure of New York is both exposed and validated by *The Age of Innocence*. Just as the machinations of the inhabitants of the Faubourg compelled the admiration of their victim, John Durham, so Newland Archer, for all his educated eye – 'He supposed that his readings in anthropology caused him to take such a coarse view of what was after all a simple and natural demonstration of family feeling'[13] – finally obeys the moral injunctions of his society in full consciousness of the manner in which he has been constrained into compliance. Both Newland Archer and May Welland have been schooled in 'an atmosphere of faint implications and pale delicacies',[14] yet Archer differentiates between himself and May in terms of the effect which their upbringing has had upon them: she is the 'terrifying product of the social system he belonged to and believed in', nurtured with the express purpose of being offered to a man 'in order that he might exercise his lordly pleasure in smashing it like an image made of snow'. Half of the sexual matrix is thus empowered and sanctioned as superior in both knowledge and freedom of choice and it is through this imbalance, no less here than in the New York of Undine Spragg, that the crucial mistake of the marginalising of the woman is discovered. The fact that May is a 'creation of factitious purity', is emphasised by the pitiless manner in which Wharton articulates the rituals and rites of 'Old New York' which have formed her. The 'young girl who was the center of this elaborate system of mystification'[15] is at once the most consummate achievement of 'nearly three hundred years of social observance' and the reason for its decease.

Wharton is able to give Archer the power to utter that which is deemed anti-social or subversive by his fellow New Yorkers because the freedoms he advocates will not be demanded by those he purports to speak for:

> His own exclamation: 'Women should be free – as free as we are,' struck to the root of a problem that it was agreed in his world to regard as non-existent. 'Nice' women, however wronged, would never claim the kind of freedom he meant, and generous-minded men like himself were therefore – in the heat of argument – the more chivalrously ready to concede it to them. Such verbal generosities were in fact only a humbugging disguise of the inexorable conventions that tied things together and bound people down to the old pattern.[16]

The fact of oppression here actually guarantees Archer's freedom of speech, the status quo will prevail; the matters which are truly challengeable in this society are never directly articulated by anyone except perhaps Ellen Olenska, whose position as an outsider provides her with linguistic privileges. Every social process – no matter how trivial – has an unspoken dimension: 'In reality they all lived in a kind of hieroglyphic world, where the real thing was never said or done or even thought, but only represented by a set of arbitrary signs'.[17] Nowhere is this unspoken dimension more evident than in Wharton's depiction of May Welland. Her character exemplifies the paralysis of a society which defines and determines certain types without allowing them to develop a consciousness of the process. Archer is forced to articulate May negatively: 'He perceived that such a picture presupposed, on her part, the experience, the versatility, the freedom of judgement, which she had been carefully trained not to possess',[18] innocence, as embodied in May Welland, is both tragic and destructive to all concerned. May has been brought up for marriage and in order to fulfil the aim of her education she can exert herself – lying to Ellen about the certainty of her pregnancy ensures that she keeps her husband – but only because Archer is willing, at the last, to be bound by the same rules that she obeys. She has not been allowed to develop any independent resources, she cannot change or develop and her extinction as a species is assured; like the 'Kentucky cave-fish, which had ceased to develop eyes because they had no use for them', she would 'look out blankly at blankness' if Archer removed 'the bandage from [her] eyes'.[19]

May features as 'a civic virtue or Greek goddess', she is 'a type rather than a person',[20] set in a pattern – 'Diana-like'[21] – with her bow and arrow, she compels admiration for her physical perfection and effortless serenity, but she is hollow and empty when sounded. Once having grown to adulthood there is no longer any expectation or, indeed, capacity for change, and it is here, in the creation of the standardised woman, that old New York constructs its own downfall. The placing of the woman at the centre of a generalised and unchanging aesthetic of 'civic virtue' has meant that society cannot grow beyond its own, outdated, formulation of perfection. As Archer makes plain at the end of the novel, when casting back to the time of his engagement to May, nothing ever disturbed her conception of the status quo:

> And as he had seen her that day, so she had remained; never quite at the same height, yet never far below it; generous, faithful, unwearied; but so lacking in imagination, so incapable of growth, that the world of her youth had fallen into pieces and rebuilt itself without her ever being conscious of the change. This hard bright blindness had kept her immediate horizon apparently unaltered. Her incapacity to recognize change made her children conceal their views from her as Archer concealed his; there had been, from the first, a joint pretense of sameness, a kind of innocent family hypocrisy, in which father and children had unconsciously collaborated.[22]

This description of May is also a description of old New York, the two are indistinguishable. The novel begins when the city is still definable by the 'sociable old Academy' and its frame of linguistic reference emphasises the fact of historical continuity even if only in terms of taboo – 'what was or was not "the thing" played a part as important in Newland Archer's New York as the inscrutable totem terrors that had ruled the destinies of his forefathers thousands of years ago'. This opening, in 'the early 'seventies', is also, however, a closure: the certainty of the imminent destruction of this society is evident in every reference which Wharton makes to an area of physical or linguistic change, such as the building of the new Opera House '"above the Forties"', the arrival of the '"new people"' and even the popularity of the '"Brown coupé"'[23] – all are thrust forward for particular attention by their enclosure within the inverted commas of the obsolete. The novel is a self-conscious final look at 'the tight little citadel of New York'[24] before it disappears, and its superannuation is simultaneous with that of women like May Welland. The woman is synonymous with the city; they have both been constructed and sustained toward the same end and for the same purpose. The vaunted straightfor-wardness of the appearance and boundaries of both, what Ellen Olenska sees as the social and topographical predictability of the city: '"Is New York such a labyrinth? I thought it so straight up and down – like Fifth Avenue. And with all the cross-streets numbered!"'[25] means that anything outside their range of experi-ence – 'the dread argument of the individual case'[26] – can only be dealt with below the level of the social or linguistic act. At the dinner party which marks Ellen's farewell to New York the power of the city and its aborigines is wielded successfully but finally: no longer will it be possible to rely upon the compliance of all, including the victim, to maintain a status quo which will not adapt to change:

> As his glance traveled from one placid well-fed face to another he saw all the harmless-looking people engaged upon May's canvas-backs as a band of dumb conspirators, and himself and the pale woman on his right as the center of their conspiracy. And then it came over him, in a vast flash made up of many broken gleams, that to all of them he and Madame Olenska were lovers, lovers in the extreme sense peculiar to 'foreign' vocabu-laries. He guessed himself to have been, for months, the center of countless silently observing eyes and patiently listening ears,

he understood that, by means as yet unknown to him, the separation between himself and the partner of his guilt had been achieved, and that now the whole tribe had rallied about his wife on the tacit assumption that nobody knew anything, or had ever imagined anything, and that the occasion of the entertainment was simply May Archer's natural desire to take an affectionate leave of her friend and cousin.

It was the old New York way of taking life 'without effusion of blood': the way of people who dreaded scandal more than disease, who placed decency above courage, and who considered that nothing was more ill-bred than 'scenes', except the behavior of those who gave rise to them.[27]

May's carefully cultivated innocence, real in so far as it prevents her from seeing beyond its self-preserving limits, is like that of society itself, incapable of overt change and forced into covertness, thereby ensuring that the 'disease', feared less than 'scandal', will prove mortal.

It is the exposure of the weakness of both creations, May and New York, by the actions of Archer and Ellen Olenska, that begins the process of destruction, despite the final affirmation of the moral values of their society by these would-be transgressors. Both the city at large and May choose to treat any threat from outside their boundaries as if it does not have an external reality, relying on the scruples of Archer, or Ellen Olenska, or even May's own children, to preserve their illusions of unity, their limited topography or 'horizon'. The positive virtues of old New York, celebrated for their worth through May – 'generous, faithful, unwearied' are, nevertheless, seen to exist in a void; the conditions of their preservation, an absence of 'imagination', and an incapacity for 'growth', are also their guarantors of destruction.

The failure of her contemporaries to fulfil their potential, articulated by Wharton in the autobiography to highlight her own achievement both as a woman and as an outsider to the 'hothouse' of intellectual privilege, is also treated in *The Age of Innocence* but to wider effect. If a woman like May, artificially moulded as 'civic virtue', cannot change then it is in the reluctance of her 'lord' to involve himself in such change that the responsibility must lie. Archer, like Wharton's friends Egerton Winthrop and Robert Minturn, cultivates an 'exquisite' leisure with his piles of the latest books from Europe and his desultory practice at law. It is again the case that the decisions made about appropriate occupations in this society are negative: 'Everyone in polite circles knew that, in America, "a gentleman couldn't go into politics." . . . A gentleman simply stayed at home and abstained'.[28] There is no true acceptance of 'virtue' in the 'civic' and that is why the woman is shaped into yet another artificial form – to hide the absence of real involvement.

Archer is also committed, by his inaction, to an aesthetic which is as sterile as his political life. The authors Wharton gives him to read, Herbert Spencer, George Eliot, Swinburne and Dante Gabriel Rossetti, give him the words with which to articulate his world but not the impetus to act. They shape an apprehension of his personal topography but only enhance his sense of non-participation: 'he saw the dwindling figure of a man to whom nothing was ever to happen'.[29] Like his fictional predecessor and namesake, Isabel Archer, in Henry James's *Portrait of a Lady*, Newland is aware of the terms of his imprisonment and no less aware of his personal responsibility for his state. As Ned Winsett tells him: 'you're in a pitiful little minority: you've got no center, no competition, no audience. You're like the pictures on the walls of a deserted house: "The Portrait of a Gentleman"'.[30] Newland Archer does, however, act positively in terms of his own and his society's highest moral principles at the place where the individual and the collective responsibility converge. As he looks back he sees that 'it did not so much matter if marriage was a dull duty, as long as it kept the dignity of a duty',[31] but he also sees that 'The worst of doing one's duty was that it apparently unfitted one for doing anything else'.[32] The price of Archer's renewal of his moral commitment to the standards and practices of his 'forefathers' is, effectively, inertia.

Like Odo Valsecca in Wharton's first historical novel, *The Valley of Decision*, Archer is a middle-of-the-road hero; he is a barometer of social and aesthetic change but fails to change himself. He figures in the 'Portrait' but it hangs in 'a deserted house', and Wharton has chosen the age of Archer's passing as the most appropriate to the purpose of her American historical novel. He is the last of the 'intelligent amateurs', those compilers of well-informed but leisurely guidebooks to a society now inaccessible to the casual tourist, and, again like Odo Valsecca, he is forced to give way to the professionals, whether architects or politicians. Where Odo was influenced by his friendship with the poet Alfieri, Archer, as he looks back over his life, takes pride in the fact of his intimacy with Theodore Roosevelt: 'He had done little in public life; he would always be by nature a contemplative and a dilettante; but he had had high things to contemplate, great things to delight in; and one great man's friendship to be his strength and pride'.[33] The only real historical figure to feature in and thus verify *The Valley of Decision* is Alfieri, the radical artist; the individual carrying that responsibility has here become the politician, and the ultimate politician, the President of the United States.

Whereas it was the artist who carried the burden of historical authenticity in Wharton's first novel and was also credited with inspiring social change in eighteenth-century Italy, it is the politician who takes America into the twentieth century. The man who greeted Edith Wharton to a state dinner with '"Well, I *am* glad to welcome to the White House some one to whom I can quote *The Hunting of the Snark* without being asked what I mean!"'[34] is memorialised in *The Age of Innocence* as a signal of the fact that 'There was good in the new order too'.[35] Despite the negative assertions with which Wharton heralded the composition of her story, it is present positive; the 'old order' has wasted men like Archer and it is left to his son, Dallas, to fulfil the possibilities only suggested by his father and his contemporaries. Something has been lost: 'the new generation . . . has swept away all the old landmarks, and with them the sign-posts and the danger-signal',[36] but Wharton directly privileges the forces of change here and in her historical texts generally; the past is an imprisonment for Archer and others like him. Early in the novel Ellen Olenska, when talking of her Aunt Medora's fads, says:

'all sorts of new and crazy schemes. But, do you know, they interest me more than the blind conformity to tradition – somebody else's tradition – that I see among our own friends. It seems stupid to have discovered America only to make it into a copy of another country.' She smiled across the table. 'Do you suppose Christopher Columbus would have taken all that trouble just to go to the Opera with the Selfridge Merrys?'[37]

American society has been too afraid to be different; it has wanted to go unnoticed, like the Archer women abroad, afraid that if they ask for anything they will be accused of vulgarity or presumption. This means, however, that change – as it inevitably must – occurs elsewhere and without the informing spirit of history; the negative assertion of the 'old order' finally denies only itself.

The fixed boundaries within which the society of *The Age of Innocence* operates are also, however, the conditions which make the story possible. In her review of Percy Lubbock's edition of the Henry James Letters, published in 1920, the same year as her novel, Wharton remembers James remarking to her, after seeing 'in Paris, a play by a brilliant young dramatist': '"The trouble with eliminating the moral values is that almost all the dramatic opportunities go with them"'.[38] Wharton's story requires that all her characters subscribe to a well-established and coherent moral code which is nevertheless under threat of subversion from one of its erstwhile adherents. In *The Age of Innocence*, for the first and last time in American history, Wharton is able to show the social structure strong and corporate enough to sustain the shock of conflict from within; the anarchic forces of Undine Spragg and others like her have not yet been unleashed upon the world. It is given to Archer, as ever, to articulate the formula which ultimately defeats him, and, again, his description could easily be applied to the Faubourg: '"The individual, in such cases, is nearly always sacrificed to what is supposed to be the collective interest: people cling to any convention which keeps the family together – protects the children, if there are any"'.[39] The novel is built upon a number of conflicts between author and subject and character and situation; these conflicts – energy-giving conflicts – are all dependent upon the existence of an accepted 'collective interest'. Wharton went on, in her review of the James Letters, to quote from James's *The American Scene*, adding her own gloss on the aesthetic benefits which accrue from a highly developed society:

> 'It takes a great deal of history to make a little tradition, and a great deal of tradition to make a little taste, and a great deal of taste to make a little art.' In other words, the successive superpositions of experience that time brings to an old and stable society seemed to him as great an asset to the novelist as to the society itself. Yet he never ceased to preach that the novelist should deal only with his own 'scene', whether American or other. . . .[40]

In the writing of *The Age of Innocence* Wharton once more satisfies James's earliest injunction to her as a writer – 'She must be tethered in native pastures, even if it reduces her to a backyard in

New York' – but she is only able to do so because she is in retrospective possession, as an artist, of those increments of 'history', 'tradition' and 'taste' laid down by a New York whose aesthetic progeny are posthumous.

The Old Maid, the novella of the 'fifties, was the first to be written and the only one without an arbitrating narratorial voice modulating between past and present perspectives. In its manner of telling the story it is the closest of the four to *The Age of Innocence* and many of the same means of expression are employed in both texts. The New York of *The Old Maid* is bound by the same standards of respectable bourgeois morality as were described and espoused by the Archer and Welland clans:

> In this compact society, built of solidly welded blocks, one of the largest areas was filled by the Ralstons and their ramifications. The Ralstons were of middle-class English stock. They had not come to the colonies to die for a creed but to live for a bank-account. The result had been beyond their hopes, and their religion was tinged by their success. An edulcorated Church of England which, under the conciliatory name of the 'Episcopal Church of the United States of America,' left out the coarser allusions in the Marriage Service, slid over the cominatory passages in the Athanasian Creed, and thought it more respectful to say 'Our Father *who*' than '*which*' in the Lord's Prayer, was exactly suited to the spirit of compromise whereon the Ralstons had built themselves up. There was in all the tribe the same instinctive recoil from new religions as from unaccounted-for people. Institutional to the core, they represented the conservative element that holds new societies together as seaplants bind the seashore.[41]

However, because its cast of characters is almost exclusively female, the mode of expression is imposed from without; there is no Newland Archer here, with his privileged male perspective, to define and analogise from within. The characters expose the limits of their society by the terms of their imprisonment, not by their predication of conditions inside: 'Social tolerance was not dealt in the same measure to men and to women, and neither Delia nor Charlotte had ever wondered why: like all the young women of their class they simply bowed to the ineluctable'.[42]

The story concerns two women of the generation of 'the 'fifties',

Delia Ralston and Charlotte Lovell, each of whom fills one of the two possible female rôles in their world: Delia is the wife and Charlotte, like Janey Archer before her, is *The Old Maid*, the reminder to all single girls of the only, terrible, alternative to marriage. Both these women are mothers, Charlotte having had an illegitimate child by Clement Spender, but only Delia, the married woman, is permitted to act upon her experience of maternity. Charlotte, in being unwed, has no power at all, not even a domestic influence; she is, like the Ralston family's Harriet Hosmer statue, 'A Captive Maiden', trapped within an appearance of maidenhood, which becomes more ridiculous with every passing year, but an appearance which she is forced to keep up or lose any claim to respectability and the means to be near her daughter.

Delia Ralston, as a wife, has been officially initiated into the mysteries of life, even if she is uncertain as to their personal import. Wharton describes in some detail the complete unpreparedness of the woman for the sudden shock of intimacy which marriage brings; having 'at most yielded a rosy cheek in return for an engagement ring; there was the large double bed ... the reminder of the phrase "to obey" in the glittering blur of the Marriage Service'. The description of the progress of Delia's married life is contained within a single, page-long sentence, from 'the startled puzzled surrender' to 'the insidious lulling of the matter-of-course' with only a brief allusion to 'embarrassed pleasure'[43] on the way. Each stage in her emotional and physical development is only distinct enough to be contained within the lesser grammatical unit, every one of which makes the end of the sentence, the point of closure, tragically inevitable.

Delia's sense of anti-climax, of confused loss, is only exacerbated by the entry of Charlotte and her daughter, Tina, into her household: 'The first sight of little Tina had somehow decentralized Delia Ralston's whole life, making her indifferent to everything else, except indeed the welfare of her own husband and children. Ahead of her she saw only a future full of duties, and these she had gaily and faithfully accomplished. But her own life was over: she felt as detached as a cloistered nun. ... Life had passed her by and left her with the Ralstons'. Wharton again uses the verb which twenty years before had expressed the emotional shock of Lily Bart's encounter with the poor girls at Gerty Farish's Girls' Club in *The House of Mirth* – 'decentralize'. The experience shifts the centre of self, the grounds upon which judgements are made and desires predicated. There is no longer anything for Delia but that 'future full of duties', Charlotte's confession having shown her at once the alternative and the terms of her own existence: 'Then for the first time Delia, with a kind of fearful exaltation, had heard the blind forces of life groping and crying underfoot. But on that day also she had known herself excluded from them, doomed to dwell among shadows'. Charlotte's revelations, even though they come from so unprepossessing a source, make clear to Delia the complete misdirection of her own life; there is no place in the Ralston house for 'plans and visions', as the family as a whole, like the society formed in its own image, relies on 'conformity', 'acquiescence' and 'concession', acts of self-negation, to supply it with 'fresh proofs of its durability'. As in the New York of *The Age of Innocence* it is given to the few to understand where such denial will lead; Delia knows that she is 'looking at the walls of her own grave',[44] but is not able to use that knowledge to any significant extent. Delia's 'grave' is also that of the Ralstons, those 'solidly welded blocks' have turned from dwelling-place into tomb.

The restrictions which operate within the 'citadel' of *Old New York* are highlighted by Wharton in her historical novels, and all the stories in the series which bears the name of the city are concerned with the individual who is out of synchronisation with his or her time. In *The Old Maid* it is ironic that this figure should should not be Charlotte Lovell, whose anti-social act provides the substance of the drama, but Delia Ralston, who is ultimately free to bend the rules of her society because she has otherwise adhered to them so faithfully. Charlotte is actually forced into an even greater conformity by her one act of rebellion; Wharton is again pressing the point that only security and certainty can provide the basis for informed and valid change whereas the Ralston refusal to adapt, to take risks, can only waste the lessons of the past.

In the novella of the 'sixties, *The Spark*, the central protagonist, Hayley Delane, stands out, for the youthful narrator, as a man not in his proper time and place: 'I could never look at him without feeling that he belonged elsewhere, not so much in another society as in another age'.[45] The story, told from the perspective of the 1890s, is concerned with Delane's past – specifically, the most important decade of his existence, the 'sixties – and the sense of that past which emanates from him. Delane, 'a New York banker of excessive weight and more than middle age, jogging on a poney across a Long Island polo field,' reminds the narrator, 'whimsical-

ly' of 'the figure of Guidericcio da Foligno, the famous mercenary
riding at a slow powerful pace across the fortressed fresco of th
Town Hall of Siena'.[46] Trivialised by his society and his connec
tions, his presence speaks of wider and more glorious achieve
ments to a mind starved of imaginative sustenance; Delane's 'littl
sporting successes' are posited 'as if, mysteriously, they were th
shadow of more substantial achievements, dreamed of, or accom
plished, in some previous life'.[47]

What the narrator sees, rather overstatedly, as the 'mystery' o
Delane is partly resolved by the discovery that at the age of sixteen
in 'the 'sixties', he had run away to fight in the Civil War and ha
been wounded at Bull Run. The intimations of martial glory an
grandeur discerned in Delane's merest action are thus substan
tiated by his actual history. This revelation, however, whils
defining the source of Delane's singularity, also proves the fact o
the insensibility of all those around him to history, national o
personal. In the notebook entry which outlines the story of *Th
Spark*, Wharton adds, in parenthesis, '(Lay stress on N.Y.'s indiffer
ence during Civil war – flight to Europe, sneers at Abolition, et
etc. It was exactly the *emigré* atmosphere into which I was born.)'[4]
The complete insularity of New York and its self-regarding code o
behaviour is portrayed both as a decline from an age wher
'substantial achievements' were thought possible, and as a betraya
of a later generation left to guess at its own history. As the narrato
says:

> That was the dark time of our national indifference, before th
> country's awakening; no doubt the war seemed much farthe
> from us, much less a part of us, than it does to the young men o
> today. Such was the case, at any rate, in old New York, and mor
> particularly, perhaps, in the little clan of well-to-do and indolen
> old New Yorkers among whom I had grown up.[49]

The New York which Wharton draws is shown to be outside th
current of both national and international concern and change, an
the narrowness of its interest – where Delane is the only reminde
of the possibility 'of times and scenes and people greater than h
could know'[50] – is brought to an even more bathetic climax b
Delane's reaction to the discovery that the man who nursed him s
faithfully when he was wounded was Walt Whitman and 'wrote al
that rubbish'.[51]

The same careful demarcation of the qualities of difference in the individuals who, by their exception to the rule, are used by Wharton to portray the limitations of an age, is also evident in the drawing of Lizzie Hazeldean in the novella of the 'seventies, *New Year's Day*:

> She had done one great – or abominable – thing; rank it as you please, it had been done heroically. But there was nothing to keep her at that height. Her tastes, her interests, her conceivable occupations, were all on the level of middling domesticity; she did not know how to create for herself any inner life in keeping with that one unprecedented impulse.[52]

In order to bring material comfort to her sick husband, who had rescued her from the humiliation of dependence upon relatives concerned to be seen to do the right thing but grudging in the smallest point of its execution, Lizzie Hazeldean employs the only asset she knows how to use, her body. She becomes, as she says – 'an expensive prostitute' – a word too straightforward for New York or the man whose mistress she becomes to utter: 'No one reproved coarseness of language in women more than Henry Prest; one of Mrs. Hazeldean's greatest charms (as he had just told her) had been her way of remaining "through it all," so ineffably "the lady"'.[53] As she is observed by a representative social sample, indulging in 'over-eating, dawdling, and looking out of the window: a Dutch habit still extensively practised in the best New York circles',[54] so she has been watched throughout her life, with interest but an interest far removed from positive assistance or intervention. No-one has enquired as to how she is to support her husband through his illness, for, despite the fact that 'New York attached no great importance to wealth', it also 'regarded poverty as so distasteful that it simply took no account of it'.[55] Like Lily Bart before her, she is under the scrutiny of the watchers of West Twenty-third Street, who wait for her to make the mistake which will allow them to condemn her at last for the poverty and friendlessness for which they are partly responsible.

Every act in this smallest of worlds is conducted in the public eye and it is not only marital or sexual transactions which are of general interest. In the novella of the 'forties, *False Dawn*, the individual who is marked out for our special attention is rejected by both family and society at large for failing to act in accordance with public taste in aesthetic matters. Sent abroad on his grand tour with instructions to return bearing a Raphael to dignify the family name, Lewis Raycie is disinherited for his espousal of the early teachings of John Ruskin and his taking of advice on purchase from, as his father describes them '"other friends; . . . a Mr. Brown and a Mr. Hunt and a Mr. Rossiter, was it? Well, I never heard of any of those names, either – except perhaps in a trades' directory"'.[56]

The Raycies are old Americans; a Raycie was a 'Signer' and the family home features 'confidently as a "Tuscan Villa" in Downing's *Landscape Gardening in America*',[57] the treatise which gave *Hudson River Bracketed* its name Mr Raycie, being a man with a keen sense of family, wishes 'to create a gallery; a gallery of Heirlooms'.[58] Not for him the indigenous artist – whether painter or writer – and Lewis's sister, Mary Adeline, has to conceal from her parents that she is caring for the destitute and ill wife of Edgar Allan Poe whom her father denounces as one of the 'blasphemous penny-a-liners whose poetic ravings are said to have given them a kind of pothouse notoriety'. Mr Raycie's aesthetic is firmly based on his bank-balance and the fact that spending power in combination with the well-established – '"Where are our Old Masters?"'[59] – is the only assurance of quality. Along with his fellow New Yorkers, who join with him in condemnation of Lewis's purchases, his basis for judgement is still 'somebody else's tradition'. Wharton based the story of Lewis Raycie upon the real figure of James Jackson Jarves, whose pictures were ultimately to form the basis of the Yale University collection, and who had met with the same measure of puzzled indifference to his espousal of Ruskin's counter-establishment movement.

The rejection of Lewis and his determination 'to go forth and preach the new gospel to them that sat in the darkness of Salvator Rosa and Lo Spagnoletto'[60] is presented here as a missed opportunity for American culture. The conversion of the collection to 'pearls and Rolls-Royce'[61] by descendants as unappreciative as Lewis's contemporaries is a simple, if bitter, human tragedy. This is dwarfed, however, by the legacy of aesthetic belatedness which old New York once more bequeaths to the coming generation; the paintings, once worthless, have become priceless, but the revolution in taste which has effected this change has happened elsewhere; the museum culture cannot demonstrate initiative but, by its own conventions, must always be derivative. Where Wharton began, with the enlivenment of her landscape by comparisons with Salvator Rosa so that the audience of *The Valley of Decision* would have a common ground of seeing – that of the tourist – she ends, in her final novel, *The Buccaneers*, with a heroine of the American 1870s whose aesthetic is formed by Rossetti's *The Blessed Damozel*, but who must become an exile if she is to live by it.

Edith Wharton's last novel, *The Buccaneers*, remained unfinished at her death. Twenty-nine chapters are, nevertheless, fully written and the complete story is laid out in a plan which was included in the published text by Gaillard Lapsley, her literary executor, who also wrote an introduction and afterword for the novel. *The Buccaneers* is Wharton's own ''Tis Sixty Years Since' and looks back over her whole lifetime. The self-conscious voice of the anthropologist which plays so important a part in *The Age of Innocence* and *Old New York* undergoes something of a change in this novel as there is no arbitrator to modulate between past and present and much less emphasis is, as a consequence, placed upon the difference between ages. A whole-historical and topographical consciousness is operating in *The Buccaneers*; the key locations in the story are freighted with both mythic and actual historical significance and the title of the novel itself contains a double sense of past meaning and present intention. The American girls 'embark together on the adventure',[62] but are out to make individual capture of wealth and power.

The women portrayed in this story are not pioneers exploring on behalf of their country, they are free-agents just as their original namesakes were freebooters; they owe no loyalty to the American community as represented by a New York which does business with their fathers but ignores them socially. As well as being excluded from social consideration they are also, however, excluded from their only chance of acquiring a real sense of their own history. In closing itself off from all contact with the outside world, except, of course the occasional stray English or Italian nobleman, old New York deprives its fellow citizens of an understanding of its traditions and their background. When Nan St George arrives in England, the accessibility of that country's history – written into every corner of the landscape and its inhabitants – is what engages her; the landscape of New York is so jealously guarded that those outside its carefully maintained boundaries have no choice but to look elsewhere or to live without a sense of the past. It is only, again, the exception to the general rule, Nan St George, who feels the lack of such a guiding spirit but she communicates, as Vance Weston could never communicate, a real need, a real sense of what it is like to live in that 'land which has undertaken to get on without the past, or to regard it only as a "feature" of aesthetic interest, a sight to which one travels rather than a light by which one lives'.[63]

Wharton moves with assurance between continents in this novel, and between native and exile, newcomer and long-established inhabitant to construct a picture unequalled in her work for its ease and also its benignity. This does not signal a loss of skill or force, as any consideration of the brilliant scene between the American girls and Lady Idina Churt at Runnymede will illustrate. What it does show is Wharton, along with Laura Testvalley, the 'little brown governess'[64] from a family of political exiles, cousin to Dante Gabriel Rossetti, deciding to:

cast in her lot once for all with the usurpers and the adventurers. Perhaps because she herself had been born in exile, her sympathies were with the social as well as the political outcasts – with the weepers by the waters of Babylon rather than those who barred the doors of the Assembly against them.[65]

The governess who has served the families of the Dukes of Brightlingsea and Tintagel and Mrs Russell Parmore of New York steers her new charges towards London when she realises that they stand no chance of acceptance among the 'knickerbocker families' of New York; 'The invasion of England had been her own invention, and from a thousand little signs she already knew that it would end in conquest'.[66] Wharton is, for the first time, outside looking in at her old New York and she extends her sympathies to the would-be 'Invaders'. In the novel closest in time to *A Backward Glance* a change of perspective gives a new dimension to the partial and reluctant identification between herself and the new money from the west in the autobiography, and a new and revivifying tolerance is the outcome.

Within the novel Wharton gives us very little direct contact with the denizens of the old city fortress, imitating the experience of the St Georges and their friends who have few opportunities to see what lies within. Instead, the insularity of the English aristocracy bears the brunt of her mockery, ignorance of America and its inhabitants being used to great comic effect in the story. The

Marchioness of Brightlingsea's telegram to her old employee, Laura Testvalley, on the subject of her younger son's engagement to Conchita Closson registers her sole concern; 'Is she black his anguished mother Selina Brightlingsea',[67] her knowledge of the American continent being based on a Vandyke conception of *The Spanish Main and the Americas*; and the Duke of Tintagel enquires of Laura, on the subject of marriage services in New York: '"Have they the necessary churches?"'.[68] The English also make the assumption that archery was taught to the Americans by the Red Indians whilst for the reader the merest glance at the deliberate allusiveness of Wharton's description of May Welland at the Newport Archery Club in the 1870s in *The Age of Innocence*, to George Eliot's picture of Gwendolen Harleth at the Brackenshaw Archery Club in her 1876 novel, *Daniel Deronda*, will confirm Wharton's emphasis on the cultural and social likenesses between continents in the nineteenth century. It is given to Sir Helmsley Thwarte – country house owner and patron of the Pre-Raphaelites – to express, in a letter to his son Guy, who is working in Brazil, the cultural limitations of both sides:

> The Duchess and her daughters are of course no less bewildered. They have no conception of a society not based on aristocratic institutions, with Inverary, Welbeck, Chatsworth, Longlands and so forth as its main supports; and their guests cannot grasp the meaning of such institutions or understand the hundreds of minute observances forming the texture of an old society. This has caused me, for the first time in my life, to see from the outside at once the absurdity and the impressiveness of our great ducal establishments, the futility of their domestic ceremonial, and their importance as custodians of historical tradition and of high (if narrow) social standards.[69]

The Buccaneers, her last work, was the first of Wharton's novels to have most of its action take place in England and the specific topography of the 1870s with its Anglo-Saxon accessibility enables her to examine modes of historiography as well as to practise it herself. The novel portrays the growth of a sense of history in Annabel St George; her education at the hands of Laura Testvalley is charted by the poetry of Rossetti – an important voice in all Wharton's later historical novels. Nan's feeling for the 'rich low murmur of the past'[70] finds both stimulus and answer in Rossetti's sensuous interpretation of legend and religious mysticism. Neither the English nor the Americans in general have an active sense of the past; only those used to exile, for one reason or another – Laura Testvalley, Guy Thwarte and Nan St George – have a true understanding of their shared, cross-cultural inheritance and this, contrarily, gives them the strength to leave behind the places to which they have the most profound attachment.

All Edith Wharton's writing is concerned with the relationships between old and new, native and exile, the land and its inhabitants. *The Buccaneers*, though incomplete, comes to terms, finally, with all that it means, of pleasure and pain, to move between countries. The cultural stability of the nineteenth century has been lost to the American and the narrow and constricting exclusivity of New York, with its equally exclusive division of society into business and home, profession and family, must bear the greatest part of the responsibility for that loss. All the cogency, or even credibility, of the moral imperatives of a nation has been dissipated by the narrowness of their expected application. This last novel, however, remains as a statement of possibility; Nan St George, at home for the first time in the country which is iconically represented by her name, feels that what the landscape has to offer can be carried with her beyond its boundaries. The close of the story is planned in this way:

Sir Helmsley Thwarte, the widowed father of Guy, a clever, broken-down and bitter old worldling, is captivated by Miss Testvalley, and wants to marry her; but meanwhile the young Duchess of Tintagel has suddenly decided to leave her husband and go off with Guy, and it turns out that Laura Testvalley, moved by the youth and passion of the lovers, and disgusted by the mediocre Duke of Tintagel, has secretly lent a hand in the planning of the elopement, the scandal of which is to ring through England for years.

Sir Helmsley Thwarte discovers what is going on, and is so furious at his only son's being involved in such an adventure that, suspecting Miss Testvalley's complicity, he breaks with her, and the great old adventuress, seeing love, deep and abiding love, triumph for the first time in her career, helps Nan to join her lover, who has been ordered to South Africa, and then goes back alone to age and poverty.[71]

Nan and Guy are united, but Laura Testvalley sacrifices her own belated chance of romantic love in order to make that union possible; the cross-cultural arbiter remains, at the last, alone.

Conclusion

Edith Wharton turned the cultural dislocations of the passage between nineteenth and twentieth centuries to her advantage as a writer; her re-orientation of the social world, in fiction and in travelogue, advanced both understanding and possibility for the artist. Her whole output – the novels and guidebooks, novellas and critical writings, to say nothing of the considerable number and range of her short stories – inter-penetrate and inform each other, making clear thematic or geographical difference yet illustrating and extending the overall coherence of her creative achievement.

In recent years there has been a resurgence of interest in Wharton's work; not one which equals the interest of her contemporary audience but one which nevertheless grows and flourishes as a new generation of readers gain access to her novels and stories. Her work not only describes national differences, it transcends them; the concerns which give cogency to her fiction are universal at the same time as specific. Wharton's vision combines the qualities which she laid as the foundations for a harmonious existence – a respect for the past and its practices in conjunction with a confident embracing of the future. It is essentially a vision that demonstrates how the necessary balancing of forces between apparently opposite elements – male and female, old and new, hope and disillusion – may be achieved; a vision that offers each reader a sense of the possibilities of place and a place from which to judge the possible.

Notes and References

INTRODUCTION

1. Edith Wharton, *A Backward Glance* (New York: 1934; rpt. London: Constable, 1972), p. 205.
2. *A Backward Glance*, p. 119.
3. Edith Wharton, *A Motor-Flight Through France* (New York: Charles Scribner's Sons, 1908), p. 1.
4. In his book *Charmed Circle: Gertrude Stein and Company* (London: Phaidon Press, 1974), p. 328, James R. Mellow tells of a conversation between Bravig Imbs and Gertrude Stein in the summer of 1928 in which Stein elaborated upon her theory 'that America was now the oldest country in the world, having entered the twentieth century earlier than other countries. Its problems, she explained, were the troubles of senility rather than of youth'.
5. *A Backward Glance*, p. 6.
6. Edith Wharton, *Hudson River Bracketed* (New York: D. Appleton & Co., 1929), p. 392.

1. THE VALLEY OF DECISION

1. Edith Wharton, 'Italy Again', MS, Za Wharton 174, Yale Beinecke Library.
2. Edith Wharton, *A Backward Glance* (New York: 1934; rpt. London: Constable, 1972), p. 69.
3. Henry James, *William Wetmore Story and His Friends* (London: Thames & Hudson, 1903), Chapter One.
4. Edith Wharton, *The Valley of Decision* (New York: Charles Scribner's Sons, 1902), p. 148.
5. Ellen Moers, *Literary Women* (1963; rpt. London: Women's Press, 1978), p. 200.
6. Gordon S. Haight, *George Eliot: A Biography* (Oxford, 1968; rpt. Oxford: Oxford University Press, 1978), p. 345.
7. *The Valley of Decision*, p. 562.
8. Elaine Showalter, *A Literature of Their Own: British Women Novelists from Brontë to Lessing* (London: Virago, 1982), pp. 43–4.
9. *A Backward Glance*, p. 128.
10. Ibid., pp. 47–8.
11. Edith Wharton, 'Fiction and Criticism', MS, Za Wharton 215, Yale Beinecke Library, pp. 9–10.
12. *A Backward Glance*, p. 128.
13. *The Valley of Decision*, p. 177.
14. Ibid., p. 565.
15. Georg Lukács, *The Historical Novel*, trans. Hannah and Stanley Mitchell (London: Peregrine Books, 1969), p. 38.

155

16.   *The Valley of Decision*, p. 582.
17.   Ibid., p. 358.
18.   Ibid., p. 636.
19.   Ibid., p. 347.
20.   Ibid.
21.   Edith Wharton, *Italian Backgrounds* (New York: Charles Scribner's Sons, 1905), p. 128.
22.   *The Valley of Decision*, p. 107.
23.   Ibid., p. 105.
24.   *A Backward Glance*, p. 67.
25.   Sir Walter Scott, *Waverley* (London, 1814; rpt. London: Penguin Books, 1972), p. 492.
26.   *A Backward Glance*, p. 6.
27.   Lukács, *The Historical Novel*, p. 57.
28.   *A Motor-Flight Through France*, p. 11.
29.   *Italian Backgrounds*, p. 170.
30.   Edith Wharton, *Italian Villas and Their Gardens* (London: John Lane, Bodley Head, 1904), p. 7.
31.   *Italian Villas and Their Gardens*, pp. 12–13.
32.   *Italian Backgrounds*, p. 177.
33.   Edith Wharton, 'Life and I', MS, Za Wharton 7, Yale Beinecke Library, p. 50.
34.   *Italian Backgrounds*, pp. 104–5.
35.   Ibid., pp. 178–9.
36.   *A Backward Glance*, p. 206.

2.   THE CUSTOMS OF THE COUNTRY: FRANCE

1.   Nathaniel Hawthorne, *The Marble Faun* (1860; rpt. New York: New American Library, 1961), p. vi.
2.   Edith Wharton, 'The Great American Novel', *Yale Review*, NS xvi (July 1927), p. 653.
3.   Percy Lubbock, *Portrait of Edith Wharton* (London: Jonathan Cape, 1947).
4.   Henry James, Letter to Edith Wharton, 4 December 1912, in Irving Howe (ed.), *Edith Wharton: A Collection of Critical Essays* (Englewood Cliffs, New Jersey: Prentice-Hall, 1962), p. 148.
5.   Edith Wharton, *Madame de Treymes* (New York, 1907; rpt. New York: Charles Scribner's Sons, 1970), p. 178.
6.   *Madame de Treymes*, p. 167.
7.   Ibid., p. 166.
8.   Ibid.
9.   Edith Wharton, *The Custom of the Country* (New York: Charles Scribner's Sons, 1913), p. 207.
10.   Edith Wharton, *French Ways and Their Meaning* (New York: D. Appleton & Co., 1919), pp. 115–17.
11.   *French Ways and Their Meaning*, p. 111.
12.   Edith Wharton, *A Motor-Flight Through France* (New York: Charles Scribner's Sons, 1908), p. 32.
13.   *A Motor-Flight Through France*, p. 5.

14. Ibid., p. 47.
15. Ibid., p. 74.
16. Edith Wharton, *The Reef* (New York: D. Appleton & Co., 1912), pp. 82–3.
17. Edith Wharton, *The Age of Innocence* (New York: D. Appleton, 1920), p. 350.
18. *The Reef*, p. 21.
19. Ibid., pp. 74–5.
20. Ibid., p. 40.
21. Ibid., p. 128.
22. Ford Madox Ford, *A Mirror to France* (London: Duckworth, 1926), p. 219.
23. *The Reef*, p. 40.
24. Ibid.
25. *A Motor-Flight Through France*, p. 177.
26. *The Reef*, pp. 23–4.
27. Millicent Bell, *Edith Wharton and Henry James: The Story of Their Friendship* (London: Peter Owen, 1966), p. 277.
28. *The Reef*, p. 319.
29. Ibid., p. 360.
30. *French Ways and Their Meaning*, pp. 101–2.
31. Henry James, 'The New Novel', (1914; rpt. in *Selected Literary Criticism*, ed. Morris Shapira, London: Peregrine Books, 1968), p. 387.
32. Edith Wharton, *A Backward Glance* (New York: 1934; rpt. London: Constable, 1972), pp. 182–3.
33. James, *Selected Literary Criticism*, p. 387.
34. *The Custom of the Country*, p. 277.
35. Ibid., p. 480.
36. *French Ways and Their Meaning*, p. 115.
37. *The Custom of the Country*, p. 208.
38. Ibid., p. 74.
39. Ibid., p. 313.
40. Ibid., p. 83.
41. Ibid., p. 273.
42. Ibid., p. 96.
43. *French Ways and Their Meaning*, p. 35.
44. *The Custom of the Country*, p. 274.
45. Ibid., p. 294.
46. Ibid., p. 208.
47. Ibid., p. 543.
48. Ibid., p. 286.
49. Ibid., p. 349.
50. Ibid., p. 195.
51. Ibid., p. 469.

3. FIGHTING FRANCE

1. Edith Wharton, *French Ways and Their Meaning* (New York: D. Appleton & Co., 1919), pp. 14–15.

2.   Edith Wharton, *A Son at the Front* (New York: Charles Scribner's Sons, 1923), p. 226.
3.   Edith Wharton, *Fighting France from Dunquerque to Belfort* (London: Macmillan & Co., 1915), p. 4.
4.   *Fighting France*, p. 58.
5.   Ibid., pp. 82–3.
6.   Ibid., p. 58.
7.   Ibid., pp. 39–40.
8.   Ibid., p. 96.
9.   Ibid., p. 94.
10. Ibid., p. 179.
11. Edith Wharton, 'Lecture at the Soldiers and Sailors' Club', TS, incomplete, Za Wharton 175, Yale Beinecke Library, p. 15.
12. Edith Wharton, *The Marne* (London: Macmillan & Co., 1918), pp. 36–8.
13. Ibid., p. 81.
14. Ibid., p. 44.
15. Ibid., p. 28.
16. *A Son at the Front*, p. 40.
17. Ibid., p. 366.
18. Ibid.
19. Ibid., pp. 410–11.
20. Ibid., p. 417.
21. Ibid., p. 423.
22. Edith Wharton, 'Tradition', TS with MS corrections, Za Wharton 151, Yale Beinecke Library, pp. 6–7.
23. 'Tradition', p. 22.
24. Edith Wharton, 'Tradition – Outline', TS with MS corrections, Za Wharton 224, Yale Beinecke Library, p. 1.
25. 'Tradition – Outline', p. 2.
26. *The Marne*, p. 44.
27. Edith Wharton, *The House of Mirth* (New York, 1905; rpt. with a new Introduction by the author, London: Oxford University Press, 1936), p. 8.

4.   INSIDE THE HOUSE OF MIRTH

1.   Edith Wharton, 'Donnée Book', Za Wharton 221, Yale Beinecke Library, p. 79.
2.   Edith Wharton, *A Backward Glance* (New York: 1934 rpt. London: Constable, 1972), pp. 206–7.
3.   Quoted from *Godey's Lady's Book*, 1859, by Jean Strouse, *Alice James: A Biography* (London: Jonathan Cape, 1981), p. 63.
4.   William Wordsworth, 'She was a Phantom of Delight', *Wordsworth: Poetical Works*, ed. Thomas Hutchinson (London: Oxford University Press, 1969), p. 148.
5.   Edith Wharton, *The House of Mirth* (New York: 1905; rpt. with a new Introduction by the author, London: Oxford University Press, 1936), p. 171.

6. Ibid., p. 8.
7. Cynthia Griffin Wolff, *A Feast of Words: The Triumph of Edith Wharton* (New York: Oxford University Press, 1977), p. 112.
8. Edith Wharton, *The Custom of the Country* (New York: Charles Scribner's Sons, 1913), p. 195.
9. *A Backward Glance*, p. 207.
10. David Graham Phillips, *Susan Lenox: Her Fall and Rise* (New York, 1917; rpt. Carbondale and Edwardsville: Southern Illinois University Press, 1977) II, pp. 441–2.
11. *The House of Mirth*, p. vii.
12. Ibid., pp. 12–13.
13. Ibid., p. 146.
14. Ibid., p. 171.
15. Ibid., p. 173.
16. Ibid., p. 171.
17. Ibid., p. 175.
18. R. W. B. Lewis, *Edith Wharton* (London: Constable, 1975), p. 153.
19. Henry James, *The American Scene* (1907; rpt. with an Introduction by Leon Edel, Bloomington: Indiana University Press, 1968), pp. 164–5.
20. Lewis, *Edith Wharton*, p. 155.
21. *The House of Mirth*, pp. ix–x.
22. Ibid., p. 25.
23. Ibid., p. 226.
24. James, *The American Scene*, p. 53.
25. *The House of Mirth*, p. 52.
26. Ibid., p. 38.
27. Ibid., p. 31.
28. Ibid., pp. 37–8.
29. Ibid., p. 298.
30. Ibid., p. 301.
31. Ibid., p. 300.
32. Ibid., p. 348.
33. Ibid., pp. 163–4.
34. Ibid., pp. 348–9.
35. Lewis, *Edith Wharton*, pp. 317–18.
36. Edith Wharton, *The Fruit of the Tree* (New York: Charles Scribner's Sons, 1907), p. 237.
37. Ibid., pp. 623–4.
38. Charlotte Perkins Gilman, 'Economic Basis of the Woman Question', 1898, collected in *Up From the Pedestal: Selected Writings in the History of American Feminism*, ed. Aileen S. Kraditor (Chicago: Quadrangle Books, 1968), pp. 175–6.
39. *The Fruit of the Tree*, pp. 182–3.
40. Ibid., p. 202.
41. Ibid., p. 281.
42. Ibid., p. 227.
43. Lewis, *Edith Wharton*, p. 159.
44. *The Fruit of the Tree*, pp. 559–60.
45. Edith Wharton, 'Fiction and Criticism', MS and TS fragment, Za Wharton 215, Yale Beinecke Library, p. 5.

46.   Edith Wharton, *Ethan Frome* (New York, 1911; rpt. London: Constable, 1976), p. 62.
47.   Ibid., p. 27.
48.   Ibid., pp. 114–15.
49.   Ibid., p. 28.
50.   Ibid., p. 33.
51.   Ibid., pp. 39–40.
52.   Ibid., p. 92.
53.   Ibid., p. 91.
54.   Edith Wharton, 'The Writing of *Ethan Frome*', *Colophon*, 11, 1932.
55.   Edith Wharton, *Summer* (New York, 1917; rpt. London: Constable, 1976), p. 125.
56.   Lewis, *Edith Wharton*, p. 396.
57.   *Summer*, p. 207.
58.   Lewis, *Edith Wharton*, p. 180.
59.   *Summer*, p. 209.
60.   Ibid., p. 221.
61.   Ibid., p. 222.

5.   THE WRITING OF AMERICAN FICTION

1.   Edith Wharton, *A Backward Glance* (New York: 1934; rpt. London: Constable, 1972), p. 147.
2.   Edith Wharton, *The Glimpses of the Moon* (New York: D. Appleton & Co., 1922), p. 21.
3.   Ibid., p. 109.
4.   Ibid., pp. 319–20.
5.   Ibid., p. 49.
6.   Ibid., pp. 214–15.
7.   Edith Wharton, 'The Great American Novel', *Yale Review*, NS xvi (July 1927), p. 655.
8.   Edith Wharton, *The Mother's Recompense* (New York: D. Appleton & Co., 1925), p. 16.
9.   Ibid., p. 97.
10.   Ibid., p. 29.
11.   Ibid., p. 279.
12.   Edith Wharton, Letter to John Hugh Smith, May 1925, Za Wharton Shelves, Yale Beinecke Library: 'It is, of course, what an English reviewer (I forget in what paper) reviewing it jointly with Mrs. Woolf's latest, calls it: an old-fashioned novel. I was not trying to follow the new method, as May Sinclair so pantingly and anxiously does; and my heroine belongs to the day when scruples existed. One reviewer, by the way, explained the title (incidentally remarking that I am always a moralist!) by saying that Kate's reward for sparing her daughter useless pain is "the love of a good man"!'.
13.   *The Mother's Recompense*, p. 71.
14.   Ibid., pp. 30–1.
15.   Ibid., p. 342.

16. Ibid., p. 255.
17. Edith Wharton, *The Writing of Fiction* (London: Charles Scribner's Sons, 1925), p. 143.
18. *The Mother's Recompense*, p. 341.
19. R. B. W. Lewis, *Edith Wharton* (London: Constable, 1975), p. 465.
20. Edmund Wilson, 'Justice to Edith Wharton', *The Wound and the Bow* (New York: Oxford University Press, 1947).
21. Edith Wharton, Za 35 and 224, Yale Beinecke Library.
22. Edith Wharton, *Twilight Sleep* (New York: D. Appleton & Co., 1927), p. 48.
23. Blake Nevius, *Edith Wharton: A Study of Her Fiction* (1953; rpt. Berkeley: University of California Press, 1961), pp. 206–7.
24. *Twilight Sleep*, p. 24.
25. Ibid., p. 119.
26. Ibid., pp. 252–3.
27. The quotation from Traherne which appears on the title page of *The Writing of Fiction* also features as Wharton's personal motto in the manuscript notebook – 'Quaderno Dello Studente', Za Wharton 215c, Yale Beinecke Library – which is inscribed 'If I ever have a biographer, it is *in these notes that he will find the gist of me. EW 1927*'.
28. Lewis, *Edith Wharton*, pp. 148–9.
29. *Twilight Sleep*, pp. 199–200.
30. Ibid., pp. 3–4.
31. Ibid., p. 61.
32. Ibid., p. 134.
33. Ibid., p. 6.
34. Ibid., p. 189.
35. Ibid., p. 138.
36. Ibid., p. 319.
37. Ibid., p. 5.
38. Ibid., p. 115.
39. Ibid.
40. Ibid., p. 354.
41. Charlotte Perkins Gilman, 'Making a Change', *Forerunner*, December 1911, pp. 311–15.
42. *Twilight Sleep*, p. 123.
43. Ibid., p. 362.
44. Edith Wharton, *The Children* (New York: D. Appleton & Co., 1928), p. 26.
45. *The Children*, p. 16.
46. Ibid., p. 23.
47. Ibid., p. 47.
48. Ibid., p. 347.
49. F. Scott Fitzgerald, Letter to Thomas Boyd, May 1924, *Correspondence of F. Scott Fitzgerald*, ed. M. J. Bruccoli and M. M. Duggan (New York: Random House, 1980).
50. Edith Wharton, *Hudson River Bracketed* (New York: D. Appleton & Co., 1929), p. 392.
51. *A Backward Glance*, p. 119.

6. 'LITERATURE' OR THE VARIOUS FORMS OF AUTOBIOGRAPHY

1. Edith Wharton, *A Backward Glance* (New York, 1934; rpt. London: Constable, 1972), p. 119.
2. Ibid., p. 6.
3. Diaries for 1905 and 1906 are held by the Beinecke Library, Za Wharton 215a and 215b and the 1908 'page-a-day' diary and 'The Life Apart' diary by the Lilly Library at the University of Indiana.
4. Edith Wharton, 'Life and I', Za Wharton 7, Yale Beinecke Library, pp. 2–3.
5. Lewis, *Edith Wharton* (London: Constable, 1975), p. 490.
6. Edith Wharton, *Hudson River Bracketed* (New York: D. Appleton & Co., 1929), p. 3.
7. *A Backward Glance*, p. 7.
8. Ibid., p. 122.
9. Ibid., p. 68.
10. Ibid., p. 6.
11. Edith Wharton, *The Custom of the Country* (New York: Charles Scribner's Sons, 1913), p. 78.
12. *A Backward Glance*, p. 5.
13. Ibid., pp. 222–3.
14. Lewis, *Edith Wharton*, pp. 228–9.
15. *A Backward Glance*, pp. 149–51.
16. Ibid., p. 121.
17. Ibid., p. 72.
18. Ibid., pp. 47–8.
19. Ibid., p. 121.
20. 'Life and I', p. 35.
21. *A Backward Glance*, p. 144.
22. Ibid., p. 68.
23. Ibid., p. 326.
24. Ibid., p. 119.
25. Edith Wharton, 'Literature' notebook (scenario), Za Wharton 25, Yale Beinecke Library.
26. *Hudson River Bracketed*, pp. 75–6.
27. *A Backward Glance*, p. 108.
28. Ibid., p. 107.
29. 'Life and I', pp. 27–8.
30. *A Backward Glance*, p. 39.
31. 'Life and I', p. 50.
32. 'Literature', p. 47.
33. Ibid., p. 18.
34. Ibid., p. 1.
35. 'Literature', pp. 2–3.
36. 'Life and I', p. 10.
37. 'Literature', p. 8.
38. 'Life and I', pp. 8–10.
39. Ibid., pp. 10–13.
40. 'Literature', p. 22.

41. Ibid.
42. *A Backward Glance*, p. 36.
43. 'Life and I', p. 36.
44. 'Literature', p. 47.
45. *A Backward Glance*, p. 55.
46. Edith Wharton, 'Summary of *Hudson River Bracketed*', Za Wharton 224, Yale Beinecke Library.
47. *A Backward Glance*, p. 5.
48. Lewis, *Edith Wharton*, p. 490.
49. Edith Wharton, *The Gods Arrive* (New York: D. Appleton & Co., 1932), p. 432.
50. *A Backward Glance*, p. 44.
51. *Hudson River Bracketed*, p. 354.
52. Ibid.
53. Ibid.
54. Ibid., p. 433.
55. Ibid., pp. 234–5.
56. Ibid., p. 236.
57. *The Gods Arrive*, p. 383.
58. Ibid., p. 117.
59. Ibid., p. 317.
60. Ibid., p. 411.

7. THE AGE OF INNOCENCE

1. Lewis, *Edith Wharton* (London: Constable, 1975), pp. 423–4.
2. Yvor Winters, *Maule's Curse: Seven Studies in the History of American Obscurantism* (1938; rpt. in *In Defense of Reason* (Chicago: Swallow Press, 1947)), p. 185.
3. Edith Wharton, *A Backward Glance* (New York: 1934; rpt. London, Constable, 1972), p. 175.
4. James Fenimore Cooper, *The Pioneers* (1823; rpt. New York: New American Library, 1964), p. 43.
5. Edith Wharton, *The Age of Innocence* (New York: D. Appleton, 1920), p. 66.
6. Edith Wharton, 'A Little Girl's New York', *Harper's Magazine*, CLXXVI, March 1938, p. 356.
7. *A Backward Glance*, p. 6.
8. *The Age of Innocence*, p. 216.
9. Ibid., p. 73.
10. Ibid., pp. 50–2.
11. Ibid., pp. 312.
12. Ibid., p. 293.
13. Ibid., p. 66.
14. Ibid., p. 14.
15. Ibid., pp. 40–3.
16. Ibid.
17. Ibid.

18. Ibid.
19. Ibid., p. 81.
20. Ibid., p. 189.
21. Ibid., p. 211.
22. Ibid., p. 351.
23. Ibid., pp. 1–2.
24. Ibid., p. 28.
25. Ibid., p. 74.
26. Ibid., p. 309.
27. Ibid., p. 338.
28. Ibid., pp. 123–4.
29. Ibid., p. 228.
30. Ibid., p. 124.
31. Ibid., p. 350.
32. Ibid., p. 354.
33. Ibid., p. 349.
34. Lewis, *Edith Wharton*, p. 145.
35. *The Age of Innocence*, p. 352.
36. Ibid., p. 361.
37. Ibid., p. 242.
38. Edith Wharton, 'Henry James in His Letters', *Quarterly Review*, ccxxxiv (July 1920), 188–202, p. 198.
39. *The Age of Innocence*, p. 110.
40. 'Henry James in His Letters', p. 199.
41. Edith Wharton, *The Old Maid* (New York: D. Appleton & Co., 1924), pp. 4–5.
42. Ibid., p. 66.
43. Ibid., pp. 14–15.
44. Ibid., pp. 128–9.
45. Edith Wharton, *The Spark* (New York: D. Appleton & Co., 1924), p. 7.
46. Ibid., p. 22.
47. Ibid., p. 27.
48. Edith Wharton, 'Subjects and Notes – 1918–1923', Za Wharton 223, Yale Beinecke Library, p. 35.
49. *The Spark*, p. 44.
50. Ibid., p. 23.
51. Ibid., p. 109.
52. Edith Wharton, *New Year's Day* (New York: D. Appleton & Co., 1924), p. 150.
53. Ibid., pp. 114–15.
54. Ibid., p. 8.
55. Ibid., p. 154.
56. Edith Wharton, *False Dawn* (New York: D. Appleton & Co., 1924), p. 99.
57. Ibid., p. 6.
58. Ibid., p. 52.
59. Ibid., p. 51.
60. Ibid., p. 79.
61. Ibid., p. 143.

62. Edith Wharton, *The Buccaneers* (New York: D. Appleton-Century Co., 1938), p. 357.
63. Edith Wharton, *A Motor-Flight Through France* (New York: Charles Scribner's Sons, 1908), p. 11.
64. *The Buccaneers*, p. 235.
65. Ibid., p. 68.
66. Ibid., p. 159.
67. Ibid., p. 91.
68. Ibid., p. 225.
69. Ibid., p. 232.
70. Ibid., p. 249.
71. Ibid., p. 358.

Bibliography

WORKS BY EDITH WHARTON

The Valley of Decision (New York: Charles Scribner's Sons, 1902).
Italian Villas and Their Gardens (London: John Lane, Bodley Head, 1904).
Italian Backgrounds (New York: Charles Scribner's Sons, 1905).
The House of Mirth (New York: 1905; rpt. with Introduction by Edith Wharton. London: Oxford University Press, 1936).
Madame de Treymes (New York: 1907; rpt. New York: Charles Scribner's Sons, 1970).
The Fruit of the Tree (New York: Charles Scribner's Sons, 1907).
A Motor-Flight Through France (New York: Charles Scribner's Sons, 1908).
Ethan Frome (New York: 1911; rpt. London: Constable & Co., 1976).
The Reef (New York: D. Appleton & Co., 1912).
The Custom of the Country (New York: Charles Scribner's Sons, 1913).
Fighting France from Dunquerque to Belfort (London: Macmillan & Co., 1915).
Summer (New York: 1917; rpt. London: Constable & Co., 1976).
The Marne (London: Macmillan & Co., 1918).
French Ways and Their Meaning (New York: D. Appleton & Co., 1919).
The Age of Innocence (New York: D. Appleton, 1920).
The Glimpses of the Moon (New York: D. Appleton & Co., 1922).
A Son at the Front (New York: Charles Scribner's Sons, 1923).
Old New York: False Dawn; The Old Maid; The Spark; New Year's Day (New York: D. Appleton & Co., 1924) 4 Volumes.
The Mother's Recompense (New York: D. Appleton & Co., 1925).
The Writing of Fiction (London: Charles Scribner's Sons, 1925).
Twilight Sleep (New York: D. Appleton & Co., 1927).
The Children (New York: D. Appleton & Co., 1928).
Hudson River Bracketed (New York: D. Appleton & Co., 1929).
The Gods Arrive (New York: D. Appleton & Co., 1932).
A Backward Glance (New York: 1934; rpt. London: Constable & Co., 1972).
The Buccaneers (New York: D. Appleton-Century Co., 1938).
The Collected Short Stories of Edith Wharton, introduction by R. W. B. Lewis, 2 volumes (New York: Charles Scribner's Sons, 1968).

WORKS BY OTHER AUTHORS

Bell, Millicent, *Edith Wharton and Henry James: The Story of Their Friendship* (London: Peter Owen, 1966).
Benstock, Shari, *Women of the Left Bank: Paris 1900–1940* (London: Virago Press, 1987).
Cooper, James F., *The Pioneers* (1823; rpt. New York: New American Library, 1964).

Dreiser, Theodore, *Sister Carrie* (1900; rpt. New York: New American Library, 1961).

Edel, Leon, *The Life of Henry James*, 2 Volumes (London: Peregrine Books, 1977).

Eliot, George, *Romola* (1863; rpt. London: J. M. Dent & Sons, 1907).

————, *Middlemarch* (1871–2; rpt. London: Penguin Books, 1965).

————, *Daniel Deronda* (1876; rpt. London: Panther Books, 1970).

Ford, Ford Madox, *A Mirror to France* (London: Duckworth & Company 1926).

Grant, Robert, *Unleavened Bread* (1900; rpt. Ridgewood, New Jersey: Gregg Press, 1968).

Howe, Irving (ed.), *Edith Wharton: A Collection of Critical Essays* (Englewood Cliffs, New Jersey: Prentice-Hall, 1962).

James, Henry, *A Little Tour in France* (1877; rpt. London: William Heinemann, 1924).

————, *The Portrait of a Lady* (1881; rpt. London: Penguin Books, 1963).

————, *William Wetmore Story and His Friends*, 2 Volumes (London: Thames & Hudson, 1903).

————, *The American Scene* (1907; rpt. with an Introduction by Leon Edel. Bloomington: Indiana University Press, 1968).

————, *Madame de Mauves* (New York: Charles Scribner's Sons, 1908).

————, *Selected Literary Criticism*, edited by Morris Shapira (London: Peregrine Books, 1968).

Kraditor, Aileen S. (ed.), *Up From the Pedestal: Selected Writings in the History of American Feminism* (Chicago: Quadrangle Books, 1968).

Lewis, R. W. B., *Edith Wharton* (London: Constable & Co., 1975).

Lewis, Sinclair, *Main Street* (New York: Harcourt, Brace & World, 1920).

Lukács, Georg, *The Historical Novel*, trans. Hannah and Stanley Mitchell (1962; rpt. London: Penguin Books, 1981).

Mellow, James R., *Charmed Circle: Gertrude Stein and Company* (London: Phaidon Press, 1974).

Moers, Ellen, *Literary Women* (London: 1963; rpt. Women's Press, 1978).

Nevius, Blake, *Edith Wharton: A Study of Her Fiction* (1953; rpt. Berkeley: University of California Press, 1961).

Olney, James (ed.), *Autobiography: Essays Theoretical and Critical* (Princeton, New Jersey: Princeton University Press, 1980).

Phillips, David G., *Susan Lenox: Her Fall and Rise* (1917; rpt. Carbondale: Southern Illinois University Press, 1977).

Scott, Sir Walter, *Waverley* (1814; rpt. London: Penguin Books, 1972).

Showalter, Elaine, *A Literature of Their Own: British Women Novelists from Brontë to Lessing* (London: Virago Press, 1982).

Staël, Madame de, *Corinne, or Italy*, trans. Emily Baldwin and Pauline Driver (London: Frederick Warne & Co., 1883).

Strouse, Jean, *Alice James: A Biography* (London: Jonathan Cape, 1981).

Trachtenberg, Alan, *The Incorporation of America: Culture and Society in the Gilded Age* (New York: Hill & Wang, 1982).

Wilson, Edmund, *The Wound and the Bow* (New York: Oxford University Press, 1947).

Winters, Yvor, *In Defense of Reason* (Chicago: Swallow Press, 1947).

Wolff, Cynthia G., *A Feast of Words: The Triumph of Edith Wharton* (New York: Oxford University Press, 1977).

Index